# LIFE'S CHRYSALIS VOLUME 2

## STORIES OF TRANSFORMATION AND THE POWER OF CHANGE

Compiled by

## MONICA KUNZEKWEGUTA

# CONTENTS

Authors without Boundaries

# LEGAL DISCLAIMER

The information and content within this book, "Life's Chrysalis: Stories of Transformation and the Power of Change Volume 2," is not a substitute for any form of professional counseling such as a Counselor, Life Coach, Psychologist, or Physician. The contents and information provided do not constitute professional or legal advice in any way, shape, or form. The advice contained herein is not meant to replace the professional role of a psychologist or any of these professionals.

All chapters are written at the discretion of and with the full accountability of each author Monica Kunzekweguta, Authors Without Boundaries or Prime Mind (Print Media for Development), is not responsible or liable for any of the specific details, description of people, places, or things, personal interpretations, experiences, stories, and narratives contained within. The compiler and publisher are not liable for any misrepresentations, false or unknown statements, actions, or judgments made by any of their chapter content in this book. Each writer is responsible for their contribution and has shared their story in good faith to help others. T

# ACKNOWLEDGMENTS

To ALL CO-AUTHORS, thank you for sharing your personal stories to encourage others. With each story shared, a life will be transformed. Our book is a powerful masterpiece for which I am truly grateful. It is so much harder to do things on our own, so this collaborative effort will mean your *Stories of Transformation* will benefit many! My heart is filled with hope that each author fulfils their purpose in life.

The book came to life because there is a need to continue bringing out the best in ourselves and others. Everyone can teach, motivate, and inspire, but there is something profound about sharing a personal story to benefit others.

Our gratitude goes to our readers, without them there is nothing to motivate us to continue to write. You are the reason we strive to do more.

Thank you.

# FOREWORD

I've always considered myself an average guy that behind the scenes has been through hell and back without anyone ever knowing the details for fear that if anyone knew, they would somehow judge me and think differently about me. Each story in this magnificently prepared manuscript of true stories has been written by powerful women and men who have generously opened their private lives to the world, not for fear of persecution but in hopes to inspire and spark personal transformation around the world. Each author has taken the opportunity to reach inside to find the stronger part of their humanness and turn their adversity into motivation and purpose. They were all changed forever and permanently transformed in the process. Due to their very uncontrollable circumstances and unwavering belief in the higher power, they were all impelled to rise from their devastating events, learn to be true to themselves and to honor their natural knowing, and work diligently to create better circumstances.

Even though there is the natural resistance to change and forgiveness, to let go of bitterness from their oppressors, they each proudly share their story of how they were able to go beyond and release the pain that held them in chains. Some orphaned, some had family deaths, some faced incurable diseases, a tragic accident, some were abducted, some survived a war and others homelessness. Under extreme situations, they reached in, grasped for hope and took personal responsibility in the face of incredible challenges. Each story is riveting and impossible to stop reading. I somehow naively think that my life events and experiences are among the most challenging until I was able to see into the lives of these authors who, through no fault of their own, have experienced devastation beyond anything you could ever imagine and came out on the other side of life.

Give yourself the amazing experience of the lives of these incredible authors ~Domenic Certa | Founder Self Achievement Network | Author Life Plan2.2

# INTRODUCTION

Transformation is defined as a marked change in form, nature, appearance, expression, or altering something's very nature. It is often viewed as complicated, but it is a natural process that involves changing your thoughts and how you communicate to yourself. Unless we share our stories, we will not change situations, touch, move or inspire anyone. Our stories have a purpose.

Book two came about because stories of transformation are endless. In this book, you will read true personal stories from authors across the globe sharing their life experiences and how it has impacted their lives and people around them. We hope that for all first time authors, this opportunity is just but the beginning of their writing journey.

There are 11 very different stories of authors sharing their personal life experiences. Some of these stories have led the authors to go through total Personal Transformation. Despite coming from a heartbreaking background, there is a common theme in all the stories, a glimpse of hope and love.

# MY DIAGNOSIS. MY INSPIRATION.

BY CHIDO NDADZUNGIRA

*You decided to live with me without my permission, and now you are part of me. You were meant for my downfall, but I turned you into my inspiration. You were meant to destroy and kill me, but I saw every reason to live because of you. You made me stronger, and you awakened in me a part I would never have known had it not been for you.*

*My relationship with you is a "love thy enemy type," especially when you know that your enemy is there to stay. Knowing your enemy prepares one for the fight or war. You took over my body by attacking my cells and by replicating yourself. While I hate being possessed by you, I decided to develop coping mechanisms to manage our relationship; as ugly as it is; we have to live together amicably. They have done a lot of research about you to find ways of eradicating you. You were known to be merciless before the invention of antiretroviral drugs (ARV). You destroyed the lives of those infected and affected if measures were not taken in a timely and consistent manner.*

*Historically, wherever your name was mentioned, it automatically meant death. Today, due to research and advances in science, many people diagnosed as positive are living fulfilling lives without you bearing a dark cloud of death over their heads. I participated in trials because it was my hope that you will cease to be one day, and no other person will live with the fear of you taking over their life. I am going to be talking about you, the HIV Virus.*

I woke up a bit nervous on that Friday morning, knowing it was the day for me to go and collect my results. Like a school pupil waiting for their GCSE/A-Level results, my heart pounded. Even with academic results, one can predict the most likely outcome based on input and effort on the day of the exam. Thus, the results are not a complete surprise. The surprise comes when you outdo your expectations, or you underperform. I had an inclination what my test results could be based on the events leading to my decision to take the test. I was being completely honest with myself by thinking that it was more likely that I would be positive than negative.

 Prior to relocating to the UK, I was in a long-term relationship with someone that I did not trust, yet my circumstances forced me to stay. If my results were to come back negative, I was going to be surprisingly happy. If positive, then that would have been a confirmation of what I had been fearfully anticipating. In the case of an HIV test, being positive is not a positive position to be in. Yet, for someone taking a pregnancy test, especially after a few years of trying for a baby, a positive result is what they will be praying for. Deep down, I wished and prayed for negative results while at the same time I consciously reminded myself of the possibility of receiving an undesirable positive result. What a position to be in? It was very difficult to be honest, draining on all levels, emotionally, psychologically, and physically. I had reached a point of no return and had to walk that journey no matter how challenging it was. Not collecting the results was not an option, even though I had entertained that idea at the back of my mind. I decided to 'tackle the bull by its horns,' so to speak, and was determined to see this through no matter what. I had to collect the results.

I had to encourage myself to be strong. I spoke to myself to gain strength before going into the consultation room to receive my results.

While attending University for my first degree, a Bachelor of Arts, I read Philosophy as one of my three subjects of choice. One of the modules in the course was Logic. I remember very well that it was nowhere near being logical. I just didn't get it. Thankfully, at this critical moment, I realized that my lecturer's efforts did not go to waste because I vaguely remembered one particular lecture. This was a lecture when we were taught that one must go through several premises before reaching a conclusion in an argument. This innate knowledge became handy as I approached the consultation room where my results were to be disclosed. In my head, I reasoned, "HIV is a virus (first premise), it may infect human beings (second premise), I am a human being (third premise); therefore, I can be infected by the HIV virus (conclusion)." By going through this process, I was trying to convince myself that by virtue of me being human, chances were, I could get the HIV virus. All logic aside, instinctively, there was a high chance I could be positive due to the long-term relationship I had maintained with someone I knew was not faithful. Don't get me wrong, the more significant part of me wanted to hear a negative result. I had an inclination to the worst outcome as a way of safeguarding myself from the shock of expecting negative results and then receiving positive results.

One has to build coping mechanisms in preparation for news that could be as life-changing as this. We all need some form of resilience, or should I say, a thick skin, especially when intuition indicates it is quite likely that the results will indeed be positive.

Such feelings are drawn from being emotionally grounded. Knowing that the relationship that I was in presented a high risk, and I was suspicious that my partner at the time could have been HIV positive. I was in a powerless position to change my situation. I was not as assertive as I am now. If I had been, I would have done something about it. During that stage of my life, I was very vulnerable, too weak and disempowered to challenge him. Our relationship started at a point in my life when I had just come out of a broken marriage. I had married my high school sweetheart, but unfortunately, things didn't work out. When this partner found me, I was not in the right headspace; I was hurting and still in shock that my marriage had broken down.

This man came to me as a wolf in sheep's clothing. This, too, is a very long story but for another day. For now, I will draw you back to when I went to collect my HIV test results. I would like to shed light on why I decided to be tested. By taking the test, I hoped that it would put my mind to rest regardless of the outcome.

The day I went to collect my results, I was not alone. Thank God, well, not really! You see, I wished I were alone, not because I did not want support but because it was my personal journey, and I wanted to walk it by myself. Unfortunately, circumstances would dictate otherwise, and my young sister was with me. I had to be open with her as to where we were going and for what reason. I could have said it was a general doctor's visit, but I chose my first step to be open and truthful about it. At that point, I did not know why I did. She wondered why I had to take the test, but I was not keen to explain it at that point. My focus was on getting my results. When we got to the hospital, I asked my sister to sit in the waiting area while I proceeded to the consultation room to receive my results.

The consultation room was a few steps from the waiting area, but it seemed as if I walked a mile before getting to the door. I could hear myself breathing, I felt the blood pulsing through my veins, beads of perspiration were forming on my forehead, and my legs were like jelly and heavy to lift. I knocked and was told to enter. I sat in a chair, and the consultant, a very nice woman, asked how I was and if the weather was good outside. I almost screamed at her that she should stop the chit-chat and get straight to the reason I was there - my HIV test results. All the while, she was looking into my eyes, and then she said, "There is no easy way of telling you this. I am sorry, your results came back positive. This means you are HIV positive. The HIV virus infects your blood." She paused, probably expecting a reaction from me, but I did not say anything, neither did I move.

My eyes were fixed on hers, yet I could not even see her. I only heard what she had just spoken, the words repeating in echoes, as loud ripples. It felt like I was in a cave, alone, dark, damp, and cold. From all the corners of the cave came voices delivering the same bad news. Time seemed to have come to a standstill. I heard nothing else the consultant said. I was in a world of my own, by myself, listening only to those results repeating. I could not see anything but darkness. I could not feel anything except numbness. It felt as though I was in this state forever; I wondered, was I in a trance or I was dead? Yes, I thought I was dead, even though that is something one will never live to share the experience. Slowly, I came back to being present and thankful that I was alive to deal with my new positive diagnosis. I was probably in the consultation room for less than 10 minutes, but it felt like an eternity. The consultant called my name and asked if I understood what it meant to have a positive diagnosis. Of course, I did.

It was during that moment she called my name that I fully came back awakened. She asked if I was ok. I thought, "What a silly question to ask under these circumstances.

Who would be ok after receiving the news that they are HIV positive?" No, I was not alright and possibly was not going to be for a very long time. Perhaps she was questioning my sanity. Had they checked my blood pressure within the ten or less minutes I was in the consultation room; I would likely have been detained at the hospital.

The consultant carried on with her duty of care by advising me that I could access

counseling if I wanted to, but I just wanted to get out of there. I had no plan or clue as to how I was going to live my life after my diagnosis. I was given an appointment to return for a review in 3 months. The medical reviews are currently every six months.

She handed me some pamphlets with information on HIV/ AIDS and on treatment, and I left. My sister was still waiting for me, and as I approached, she stood. I do not know how I managed to smile; she seemed eager for me to give her good news.

She said, "So you are negative?" I said, "No, I am positive." She could not believe me because my smile was deceiving. I repeated myself, and she broke down and cried uncontrollably. I quickly put on my big sister's hat and began to comfort her. I wondered if she was the one who had received the HIV positive results, or if it was me? Nonetheless, her reaction was normal because it was devastating news. It's amazing how the big sister's caring streak kicks in even when I wanted and wished to be reassured that I will be fine. In reflection, if I had come out from the consultation room in pieces, who was going to comfort who? I just had to be the stronger big sister even though I was breaking down, crumbling, and crushed inside. I was looking forward to an opportunity where I would be able to let it all out by screaming or crying. From the moment I received my results, my blood was boiling. My whole body felt hot; it was as though the virus was running havoc all over my body, and I could visualize my cells trying to fight the virus but losing. One part of me wanted to run away somewhere, hoping to outrun the virus and leave it behind. I was going through all those emotions while at the same time calming my sister down. I told her in the most reassuring voice that I was not going to die but to live.

I decided to live and never to let the fear of death overshadow me. I made this decision from the onset. The days that followed were not easy. I had to continue going to work; I was a high school teacher at one of the inner London schools. As a single mother, all the bills were on me, so I did not have the luxury to sit down and feel sorry for myself. As I carried on with my day-to-day life, it seemed as if everyone who looked at me knew about my diagnosis. I was conscious that I was fortunate to be diagnosed in the UK, a country advanced in this medical field, unlike my country of origin, Zimbabwe. At the time of my diagnosis, there were negative perceptions, myths, and people discriminated against those diagnosed with HIV in Zimbabwe. Many people lost their lives because testing was not performed early enough, and access to medical interventions was not sought after due to fear of being stigmatized. Fortunately, progress has been made since then.

One day as I lay on my bed, I decided to let my son know about my diagnosis. Most people struggle with this, and it was not easy for me either. My son was about nine years old by then. I had to find the appropriate words, time, and place to have this conversation with him.

It was the most challenging thing I had to face. The consultant had suggested that someone else could deliver the bad news to him, but I preferred to do it; he is my son. When the time came, it was emotional, he cried his heart out, and I cried with him. As he sat on my lap, I allowed him to cry it out. I could not imagine what was going on in his head, but I reasoned that he probably thought his mother would die. I am his only rock. His father was not involved in his life after our marriage broke down. I held my son close; when he finally stopped crying, I reassured him that it did not mean I would die. This was followed by an explanation in simple language what HIV was and what it means to be HIV positive. I used my past teaching skills. The days, weeks, and years that followed were not always easy, but it helped our discussions once I had opened up to him.

My diagnosis was not a barrier but a turning point, a stepping-stone into my new life. The diagnosis had actually brought a more positive perspective to my life that I did not have before. It all started with me thinking I may not have long to live. I automatically felt a sense of urgency that I had to do as much as I could within the limited time that I thought I had left. I sought forgiveness, and I forgave those who had wronged me, even without them asking for it. I made the decision that I wanted to live a stress-free life filled with positive vibes. This is much easier said than done, though. Some days I would find myself crying, asking God, "Why me?", but soon I accepted this new status was here to stay. I read a lot on HIV medical research and understood how treatments were progressing. It empowered me to gain knowledge about my enemy which placed me at a vantage point. Gaining knowledge and understanding of HIV put me in a position where I was more in control of my new life and allowed me to make informed decisions on when to start treatments. I volunteered for trials because I wanted to help find ways of tackling the HIV virus. That which could have led to my stress, depression, unhappiness, and pain started to become my source of strength. My strength came from accepting the diagnosis, from disclosing to people close to me, and supporting others in similar situations. I reached a point where I was not worried about what people would say if they knew I was HIV positive. It was then that I became a free person. My disclosure in the first instance was for a selfish reason. I wanted people close to me to know so they would not be standing around my hospital bed gossiping about what I could be suffering from, but rather for them to focus on wishing me well. This was when I thought being HIV positive automatically meant one would fall seriously ill and be hospitalized. This was a common narrative during the late '90s for people in my country of origin. To most people, being HIV positive should lead to falling seriously ill, developing AIDS, followed by a painful death. At a later stage, my disclosure was more inclined to raising awareness, dispelling myths, challenging discrimination and stigmatism, and educating. The disclosure was a part of my healing even before starting on antiretroviral medication. I had nothing to hide from anyone. After each disclosure, I quickly realized that I had to offer counseling to the person I had just disclosed to. As a teacher/social-worker, I had all the skills to enable me to provide support. More importantly, I was living with this virus and getting to know it better. I continued to educate people about HIV and AIDS. By doing this, I realized a strength in me that I would have never known had I not been diagnosed positive. While counseling, I realized that whatever I was saying to others, I also spoke to myself. The counseling I offered each time I made a disclosure healed my soul and removed my fears of the virus.

When I moved to the UK, I had a university degree and a postgraduate certificate in

Education which allowed me to find a teaching job. Back in my high school days, I was not among the smartest pupils. Following my diagnosis, I decided to do something that I never imagined I could; I applied for a Doctoral study. I laughed at myself because I knew what I was capable of academically; still, I never imagined at any point that I would dream of studying towards a Doctorate. I was determined not to allow my diagnosis to be a barrier to my dreams but for it to be my inspiration.

Five years following my diagnosis, I registered for a degree at one of the Universities in London and, after three years, successfully completed my studies. After that, I went on to study towards my master's degree in Social Work, which I also successfully completed after two years. Then I challenged myself even further, applied for a Ph.D., and was ecstatic when I received an acceptance. At this point, I said to myself, 'whatever else happens, I will rightfully and confidently declare that HIV, although you are living in me and with me, you are not welcome to possess my body or mind, I am still in control of my life.' I decided to turn my life around even with the shadow of a diagnosis hanging over me. I was motivated because I wanted to prove to myself that the diagnosis of HIV was not going to stop me from chasing my dreams. The HIV positive diagnosis awakened me to things I would have never known about myself. My diagnosis became a source of inspiration because I became motivated to achieve my new goals. I was transformed forever! My life approach is more positive now, and I will never be the same person I was before the diagnosis.

Chido Ndadzungira is a qualified, registered Social Worker within a Community Learning Disability Team. Her role involves working with other professionals in empowering vulnerable adults and their families to meet their assessed needs and outcomes. Prior to her Social Worker career, Chido carried out research exploring women's views with learning disabilities on sexual relationships. Before relocating to the UK in 2001, she worked as a secondary school teacher in Zimbabwe. She continued as a secondary school teacher of Religious Studies in the UK in inner London Secondary Schools and was also a Religious Studies GCSE examiner for Edexcel and OCR. Outside her busy work life, she is a single mother of one. She enjoys writing short stories, inspiring people around her to reach their destiny or potential, listening to music, dancing, cooking, traveling, and knitting. Chido believes in enjoying everyday life regardless of the challenges that one may face.

Connect with Chido:

Twitter: @chido_nda

LinkedIn: Chido Ndadzungira.

Facebook - https://www.facebook.com/chido.ndadzungira

# TRANSFORMATION; EMPLOYEE TO ENTREPRENEUR

BY NOMSA MAROMO

**Refuse to Settle**

For the longest time I dwelled in the most dangerous place on earth and maybe you are in that spot too. Can you guess where that place could be? It's this place of contentment, connection, and predictability called the COME-FORT-ZONE. Whatever comfort zone you are currently in, you need to get out. Comfort zones prevent us from improving and they stop us from pursuing our dreams and make us miserable.

In 2000, my family moved to the USA and I studied accounting before immigrating to Canada in 2004. For many years prior to coming to North America, I worked for an international bank, Barclays PLC. My husband is a mechanical engineer and worked for one of the biggest mining conglomerates in the world, this afforded us international tuition in America. Once we were in Canada, our opportunity became a double tragedy, my husband could not find a job in his line of work, and I could not secure an articling position with any of the local accounting firms, so I settled for an entry-level position in banking. I also continued my training and completed a Bachelor of Commerce Financial Services degree, thinking this would set me apart for promotions, but it did not.

I found a solution by switching banks to accept higher positions, but it was not fulfilling. Frustrated, I started taking courses again in preparation for a CPA designation, all while continuing my search for better opportunities. Fortunately, or so I thought, I got a commercial account management position with another bank. The money was good, comparable to entry-chartered accounting remunerations, and my accounting background became handy in performing my duties, so I put my dreams on hold.

Shelving your dreams to build someone else's, is the last thing anyone should do, ever! I do not know your comfort zone but mine was a pay cheque, benefits, a bonus and an assistant. That was living the dream in my own limited world and before I knew it, I settled to conform, afraid of losing my security. Rather than exploring the uncertain fear keeps us paralyzed and tied to a situation, which is often not ideal for our growth. The saying, "Better known evil than the good yet to come" perfectly describes that way of thinking. However, understanding our fear is the first step to leaving behind the problems of the comfort zone. It might mean learning new things and taking risks, but you should just go for it.

**Not on The Payroll**

On the afternoon of Saturday September 26th, 2015 just minutes after dropping off a relative at a wedding party, another driver T-boned my vehicle. The two airbags deployed as they should but left bruises on my arms, left knee and shin. God gave me another chance because I escaped that nasty accident with no broken bones and not much injury, or so I thought. I was transported to the emergency room and spent four hours under observation. Two days later my body ached everywhere, especially within my lower back and neck areas and a swollen left knee. I was on treatment for several months, but it seemed to get worse. Now here I was, injured, hurting emotionally but nobody seemed to care. My boss disliked how I would take even an hour to go for therapy, so my future's security was on the line. Several months into therapy, my team of doctors asked me for the second time, to take time off and focus on healing, but my excuse was how important my job was to my family. Reality hit when my family doctor said "Nomsa, that job will always be there, even when you are gone. You will be replaced before your burial, but your family will have lost you."

Perhaps you question why I had not taken time off work since the accident; I thought I was safeguarding my job. I had survived two retrenchment episodes and had witnessed some of my colleagues being laid off. I thought I was safe, and I had developed an arrogant sense of belonging and entitlement.

My doctor and I agreed on a treatment plan, and he instructed me to communicate the news to my boss. Here is how that conversation went.

Nomsa: "I have not been well; you remember I was in that car accident last year in September?"

VP: …. (pause), "Yeah so…?"

Nomsa: "I have to take some time off to focus on healing."

VP: "How long will you be gone for and starting when?"

Nomsa: "I am not sure how long, but my doctor recommends, I start immediately."

VP: "So what will I do with your portfolio?"

Nomsa: …. (pause), "I don't know." [According to the boss, my clients were more important than my health hence, no empathy in his responses. It was clear that I was jobless whenever I came back, my employer (the bank) was paying my position not me, I was just a number and numbers are never sick.]

Upon my return to work on June 13th, 2017, my life was a living hell; clearly, I was being pushed out of my position. There was a new VP and, for some reason when we first met, he seemed angry with me and never spoke about my illness. From day one he complained about my poor performance, saying my numbers were the lowest in the base. Indeed, they were the lowest, because I had been away for six months on sick leave. In fact, I was performing better than some of my peers, but because he refused to prorate my scorecard, it appeared as though I had only made a single sale in eight months, yet I was pacing 150%.

I used to cry, until I realized that he was having fun and enjoyed putting me down. He started making unreasonable requests reprimanding me for work, which should have been done while I was on sick leave. I was gutted when I discovered that a colleague who took care of my portfolio during that time was unethical and had taken some of my high-level clients, and.... gotten away with that unprofessional behavior, backstabbers!

I toughened up and reminded him that I was being targeted because I took time off to heal.

The abuse became more brutal and intense as they were creating paper trails for constructive dismissal. He procrastinated in providing an ergonomic chair up until I left. I fought back and lost for the most part, but my focus was on getting a severance package. I had sleepless nights, hated going to work and carried this heavy stress on my shoulders. The painful mental torture and condescending attitude went on for four months, but it seemed more like a year and my husband wanted me to quit. My Psychologist from the accident helped tremendously, he told me that I needed to realize that my health and life was more important than the job because it can never be replaced. On Wednesday September 28th, 2017 at 10am, the VP came into my office unannounced with a brown envelope and a little pack of Kleenex. He was unusually nice and tried to pull the rapport card and I ignored him. I read the letter and immediately got up and danced. I yelled "thank you Lord". It was an offer for a severance or be dismissed if I did not meet some ridiculous unrealistic target within 30 days. I called it a threatening package since I was threatened to leave.

He placed the tissues on my desk, and I pushed it back towards him implying that there was no room for entertaining his fake empathy. He blushed, forced a fake smile, and said, "I am glad you are taking it as a joke". I asked him if all that humiliation and mental torture was necessary and he foolishly replied, "I did what I was told to do" but he never made eye contact. It was apparent that I had repossessed my power and was no longer this abused defenseless employee at his mercy. Imagine guys, I had no boss, I felt that load getting lighter and it felt so good, but I had just lost my job. Banking was all I knew besides a few odd jobs that I did when I was in university. I had ignored all warning signs of what could become of me if I stayed comfortable in building someone's dream. Now I was discarded like an old pair of shoes and felt inadequate and useless, what a betrayal? It broke my heart because I was vulnerable and weak, with only a few years before retirement, I really needed my job. Although I have scars and lost several battles during the torture, I had won the war. They failed to terminate me without a severance, you could say, I had the last laugh. It took time to come to terms with my fate, but the only person to blame was myself.

## A Blessing in Disguise

I contemplated going back to school for a master's program in Psychology Counseling, nothing to do with financial services. My family was there for me as always but did not support the idea of going back to school. Obtaining a third degree would not help soothe my anger. Our son, Mukai, who has been an entrepreneur since his late twenties, advised me for the 100th time that I needed to find something that I liked and pursue as an entrepreneur not as an EMPLOYEE. He encouraged me to build something of my own to speed up the healing process. Mukai said, "Mum, an employee's goal is the next promotion which they may never see". That sounded strange coming from my son, but it was the truth I needed to hear. The thought of me owning a business spooked me but the thought of constructing a new resume, looking for a job and being interviewed by a 30 year old HR Manager who would tell me that I am over qualified (a nice way of saying I am too old) for the position spooked me even more. Being kicked out was a blessing in disguise, it was time to make lemonade from the lemons I got. Suddenly I could do what I wanted without having to ask for permission from anyone. Sometimes I wonder about the pain we inflict on ourselves without knowing.

My transformation journey had just begun, but was I ready to destroy my inner employee to become an entrepreneur? Now my goal was the journey ahead, a process that is built upon each achievement, each failure and each lesson learnt. The fact that I would be responsible for everything, good and bad, made me grind my teeth. My new definition of security was, taking calculated risks and to me that meant failure and I was scared. Michael Jordan said, "I have failed over and over in my life, that's why I succeed," this is true, but easier said than done. Instead of focusing on my vision, I started blaming myself for why I failed to discover the entrepreneur inside me. I struggled with feelings of powerlessness and lack of confidence in the face of the new challenges.

**Service Above Self**

An old friend introduced me to my first business venture which I dumped because it was not fulfilling, and it cost our friendship. It was a Multi-Level Marketing selling expensive technology bracelets that were supposed to monitor vital signs. I sold to a few people because I wanted money and that was when I was in the selfish "me first" phase. My Purpose took time to rekindle because in the beginning it was all about me, more of revenge than dreaming, and acting big. I know we are all sent here on earth to serve others, and not to serve ourselves. As a Rotarian, I value the Four Way Test, which says; of all the things we think say or do - Is it the TRUTH?

Is it fair to all CONCERNED?

Will it build GOODWILL & BETTER FRIENDSHIPS?

Will it be BENEFICIAL to all concerned?

It did not sit well with me when I was selling something that was not a necessity and leaving people worse off financially than when I met them. The bracelet business did not pass the four-way test and it felt right to walk away. My health and emotion had improved significantly and eventually I began to feel confident focusing on how I want to serve people without hurting them. Although I appeared to be ready to start something, I had no clue what kind of business to embark on.

## When the Student Is Ready the Teacher Arrives

In May 2018, three months after losing money to the technology bracelet business, a family friend introduced us to a company that is integrating financial education with financial services for middle-income families. Initially, I had doubts because I thought it was banking and it brought a bad test in my mouth. This company has taken financial literacy, Insurance, Banking, and Investments, under one umbrella. It is giving people the best-unbiased options based on every company under their platform. The opportunity almost passed me by because I perceived myself as someone who knows everything about how money works considering my educational background and prior work experience. I needed new skills to broaden my knowledge base, so I continued to look for opportunities to learn and grow by reading books and taking courses related to the business. Entrepreneurs are constantly learning, and it is important to pursue a wealth of relationships. I surround myself with positive minded people who support me versus those who tell me what I cannot do. Surprisingly, some of the people whom I find to be non-supporting are family and friends, and it's hard to stay away from them. Spending longer hours learning and training left me always tired, so I created a ritual to stay energetic. I followed my schedule religiously avoiding distractions like Netflix, but it was difficult to leave behind old habits. I was not as relentless in pursuit of the dream as I should have been, and I took everything for granted and even contemplated quitting, but I learned to focus on where I want to be, not the current situation.

## Challenges Happen for Us, Not To Us

For me, the journey continues. At the time of this writing, the world is dealing with a global pandemic. Lockdowns and social distancing policies like those we have never experienced before. No doubt the 2020 COVID-19 pandemic has pushed many people out of their comfort zone. We salute and thank all the health care and frontline service workers for their dedication to helping others in these trying times. People have lost jobs, the stock markets are a nightmare, and much uncertainty abounds everywhere, but while this is going on it's not the cancellation of the future. It might be different from what we know, but we need to be prepared and be ready for what the future brings to us. Now is not the time to focus on pain even if it demands to be felt, ignore it, and focus on all the reasons why you will win when this is over. Bad things happen for us, not to us. We must toughen up because tough times don't last but tough people do. I always associated job loss without warning to the private sector and believed that government jobs were safer. Now even governments have shut down and this may happen again in the future. It is now clearer than ever that there is no such thing as job security. It is a misconception of people who do not want to carry the responsibility of being entrepreneurs and this resonates with me. It was the reason why I procrastinated in starting a business earlier in life. People no longer work in jobs for 30 or 40 years anymore. The landscape has changed drastically. The way we work will never be the same. Many hardworking employees are now suffering financial hardships through no fault of their own. People will recover physically and emotionally but may still be hurting financially for much longer. Fifty-three percent of Canadians live from pay cheque to pay cheque and that is why there are so many government programs to assist, otherwise people would be broke? Now we all know that anything can happen to any organization across the globe. I am not trying to instill some unreasonable fear in you, but rather highlight the importance of safeguarding yourself against job loss.

Familiarize yourself with different kinds of income. Active income is for employees, they must work to get paid and many have to work overtime or several jobs to make enough. Passive or residual income will always work for you, even if you are not actively doing the labor. It's best described like a tap you open and leave running. Initially, there is nothing passive about it until you have put in some groundwork. Then you will begin receiving the rewards of your efforts. Be careful, to not settle for being an employee or being self-employed. It's easy to find yourself working like a slave and still counting the pennies. You need to have more than one stream of income, work smart. The idea is to avoid putting all your eggs in one basket, start by having a job and a business on the side. If you are capable, start building a business full time if your situation is conducive. Find your purpose. It is time to take control of your pay cheque to achieve your financial freedom. It should be God and you in control of your destiny, not your employer, the government, or your bank. This is a call to action for everyone to embrace change and have a vision of where you are going with your life. Charles Darwin in 1809 said, "it's not the strongest of the species that survives, nor the most intelligent but the most responsive to change."

Will it be fun? No

Will it be easy all the way? Not all

Is it worth it? Yes!

Is the pain temporary? Yes (short-term pain for long-term gain)

Will you reach your goals right away? No

Will you reach your goals eventually? Absolutely!

Will you give back? I hope so, it is very fulfilling.

While I still have pain and emotional scars from the accident, I am a different person now and embrace every opportunity that helps enhance my healing process. I am forever grateful that I got an opportunity to write a chapter about my transformation journey. This has been a revelation of how bundled up I was with the injury and the unfair treatment I got at work leading to losing my job. I still have a long way to go with healing and fighting for my financial freedom, but it is bearable because I am married to the most wonderful supporting man on earth and have the best cheerleading children anyone can ask for. This journey would not have been easy without my husband's full support both morally and financially, he is my technology guy. I am so glad I found this opportunity; it is opening doors for me to change my family's legacy for generations to come.

Born in Zimbabwe, married to Daniel, has three children and three grandsons. She moved to the USA in 2000 to study Accounting at UNC Charlotte before moving to Canada in 2004 and holds a BCom Financial Services degree from Nipissing University ON. Nomsa is a Certified Financial Professional and avid campaigner for financial literacy with WFG. She is on a mission to provide North American families with better financial understanding using unbiased options to financially EMPOWER them. She has many years of work experience in banking, over a decade with Barclays PLC an international bank and an equal amount of experience with top 3 Canadian banks; Scotia, TD Canada Trust, and BMO in Retail, Small business and Commercial banking.

A firm believer in God and in giving back to the community through service above self; current member, past Vocational Director and Past President of Rotary Club of Edmonton Southeast and an avid international traveller.

Email: maimaromo@gmail.com

Facebbok: https://www.facebook.com/MaiMaromo

Linkedin: https://www.linkedin.com/in/nomsa-maromo-b1607b37/

# HEALING FROM THE INSIDE OUT

BY CAROL SIZIBA

**Refuse to Settle**

I sat at my kitchen table looking out the window as my mind raced. I was wondering which part of my life journey I should share. All kinds of thoughts flooded my mind as I debated why one part of the journey might be better than the other.

I searched through my journals questioning which experiences I would be most comfortable sharing. Then I heard a gentle voice inside my head say, 'share that which is the most uncomfortable to share because that is when you will see how well you have done on your healing journey'.

I discovered a process in my life that brought the most significant healing from my childhood traumas. I was raised in a Christian home with strong biblical values but that made it more confusing for me to understand the difficult experiences I went through. Being raised Christian and knowing the Bible verses and having a relationship with God are different concepts. What I learned, as I got older is that a meaningful relationship with God is the foundation of healing. The experience of getting to this understanding created a great internal havoc for me, and yet brought about so much healing.

The journey to having a meaningful relationship with God began a battle in my mind even while I was coming to understand God's love and forgiveness. This struggle was the longest, hardest, draining, and most devastating part of my journey. The core of who I am was birthed from this most painful part of the journey. Healing the emotional, mental and spiritual pain had to start from the inside and flow outside.

## Grief and Loss

March 24, 1976 is a day that changed my life forever yet at the time; I didn't even know the impact of that change. It was on that day that my parents died immediately upon impact when a drunk driver hit them. I was only three years old and had no clue what had just happened, or what it meant. I remember being at our house in Kambuzuma Township (in what is now Harare, the capital of Zimbabwe). I was sitting outside the chicken coop on someone's lap. I recall hearing the people singing church songs, but personally have few memories of my parents except what people have told me and I was kept from attending their funeral.

After the funeral, my siblings and I went to live with my aunt and her children. I do not remember ever sharing my grief and the loss of my parents. People would often refer to them and say how sad they felt about us children being left orphans at such a young age and felt sorry for us. I have no recollections of ever sharing my own feelings about the loss of my parents or anything else for that matter, not until well into my adult life.

As anyone can imagine, when a family is faced with such a loss and there are young children involved, things get a little sticky. Emotions run high and extended family dynamics play out. Hurt feelings can easily result in division amongst family members and damage relationships. This certainly affected my three-year-old brain and I grew to be an adult with these experiences embedded in my mind. I grew to be an adult with these fractured relationships between extended families that did not necessarily have my best interest at heart. These experiences became embedded in my brain and impacted my own connections with relatives as an adult.

I could not reconcile this principle of an all-loving God who allowed my parents to die leaving us orphans at such a young age. How could God who is so magnificent and all-powerful, allow so much pain? As a child, I only knew my life had changed and would never be the same. This made me lack a good sense of belonging due to a combination of issues. The main one was family members fighting about various decisions that impacted me.

## Subtle Pain

So much happened in bits and pieces throughout my young life that I did not comprehend, articulate nor could even acknowledge it as pain. For example, I was constantly sick with tonsils that needed to be removed but because of the extended family dynamics, it was difficult for decisions to be made about me having this surgery. There was fear about who would take the responsibility if I died during surgery. So instead, I stayed in physical pain for years and life carried on with me being in and out of the hospital. I would miss school all the time and would go to work with my aunty. She was a teacher for children with diverse abilities. I recall her making a little spot for me on the floor in the classroom and I would sleep there while she worked with the students, and I played with them whenever I was able. The children from her classroom became my friends. I had neighborhood friends, but my connections were mostly with my Auntie's students. Eventually, my Aunt made the decision for me to have the surgery realizing how much I was suffering.

After my tonsils were removed, I went back to school where I now tried to build new friendships. I never did go back to my aunt's work, never said good-bye to those friends and I never talked about the surgery, life just carried on.

Even though the tonsils caused me physical harm, how that illness was handled caused me greater psychological and emotional distress. I did not understand why all the fuss about me having the surgery. In retrospect, I thought, 'if my parents were alive' this would have been handled differently because they would not need permission from anyone, they would just make the decisions. Nevertheless, the decision was eventually made after a long-time suffering and then life settled into some normalcy with me attending school, slowly making friends, and becoming free from hospital visits.

## Transition from City to Village: Dark period of abandonment

My aunt cared for me in such a special way during my illness and after my parent's death, she became the mother I knew. She loved me and cared for me for years in special ways that to this day I still remember. I have fond memories of her making mashed potatoes for me because I could not swallow easily due to the tonsils. She would make all kinds of special food for me. I did not do as much housework because I was always sick, so I suppose I can say; I received special treatment. Knowing all she had done and how she had loved me, made it even harder to understand when the decision was made to transition me from her care to my grandmother at Arnoldine Mission.

Only the adults in my life made decisions. This transition meant moving from the city to the rural village of Arnoldine Mission to complete my elementary education there. What made this transition more difficult is that no one told me about it. No one explained anything about this transition. It just happened, just like that. I felt abandoned. One might say this practice was normal within the culture, but it does not make it any less traumatic. The feelings of abandonment were real and devastating for me. I truly felt like an orphan not worthy of explanation about anything. Instead "things" just happened to me without discussions.

It was a standard practice that every school break all the cousins went to Arnoldine, my grandparent's homestead. We would all gather there for about three weeks during the school break. It was lots of fun for a child; it was like a reunion three times a year without the parents. Just the grandparents and all the cousins. On one of those particular breaks when time came to go back home, everyone left except me. I was told by my grandmother that I would not be returning, instead I would be completing grade six and seven at Arnoldine school.

Being left behind without explanation left me emotionally paralysed. I did not understand what just happened. I lived there for about one year but that period in my life marked a significant dark moment. Failing to understand why I was left behind, I wondered how my aunt felt about me. I felt rejected, unwanted and not worthy of an explanation. I did not have closure, and so many questions left unanswered, such as could I even visit her or not? I adjusted the best I could and accepted that this was my new reality. I never really saw my aunt again until several years later when I was an adult.

Eventually, my sister (Tsitsi Rukunda-Mutepfa, who is now deceased), found a place for me at a boarding school. I recall the day I left Arnoldine, it was cold and raining and I traveled in total silence. Arriving home in Kambuzuma, my sister poured me a bath and rubbed Vaseline on my skin to get me warm. After she fed me, she then sat down and explained that my aunt had gotten married, so the decision was made to have me stay with my grandparents to allow her time to build her marriage.

She then continued to explain the plan moving forward and assured me it was going to be okay. My sister would talk to me like a person. For the first time in my life, someone took the time to talk and not just do things that I did not understand. From that day, we formed a strong bond and I liked how I felt when I was around her. She became the mother to me in the absence of my biological parents and my aunt who had taken that role for a while. She was a mother, my sister and my best friend. She treated me differently and talked about everything that had to do with my life. Even as an adult our bond remained strong until she passed on. The day she died I got a chance to have closure with her which I greatly appreciated because it allowed me closure that I had not always had the opportunity to have in the past.

Transitioning from my aunts to my grandmothers without explanation was the most devastating of all for me on so many levels. I struggled to understand how I had been so loved and cared for by my aunt from one minute to being left at the village with my grandmother the next minute. With such deep-seated regrets, that I did not get to say good-bye to my aunt or the few friends that I had made after surgery, I thought even God had left me and could not reason why.

## Questioning God

Growing up I recognized a tradition that whenever difficult situations arose the women from the church and my aunties would gather for prayers, at times this went on for hours. Therefore, I was accustomed to prayers, but did not always understand why we pray so much to this God who allowed my parents to be killed and left us orphaned.

Through this confusion, I began to question the notion of God's love; to me it felt like love could be taken away at any time without warning, so it became easier to-not become attached, because I could lose it all in a blink of an eye.

I loved my parents. Even at the tender age of three, I could sense their love and accepted it. I knew my aunt loved and accepted me too. My aunt's students showed me kindness and acceptance and so did the friends I made after surgery. All these experiences put my brain into a state of chaos. After a while, I became conditioned to people being taken from me without warning such that my heart became hard like a protective shield of steel that I had put up.

I had such difficulty reconciling this great love of God with the reality of my experiences and I continued living in this state of confusion for many years.

I lacked a sense of belonging and was in a constant state of questioning; who was this God that I grew up praying to? Supposedly, He was an all-loving God yet I had a hard time understanding the meaning of life, given so much loss. It was challenging to open up to love out of the fear of being hurt.

As an adult, looking back, I would like to believe that I could have understood the concept of loss, but I reason that it was the lack of closure alongside the voids of opportunity to share my feelings that had the greatest impact on my life.

## Transition from Zimbabwe to USA

I attended boarding school for about two years before arrangements were made for me to move to Dayton Ohio, USA with my adoptive parents. This time, my sister, Tsitsi arranged for me to have a party where I was able to say good-bye to family and friends. I appreciated this opportunity to experience closure on this part of my life. I was now going to live in a safe environment where I could feel loved and cared for, even though at the time I was still reluctant to open up to the concept of giving and receiving of love.

After moving to Dayton, I began to process my feelings of rejection and tried to understand how love could be taken away so abruptly with no explanation. It was even difficult to believe that I could question these events because it made me feel ungrateful for having been cared for after my parents' death. I still did not feel that I could share openly the complete impact of the actions of the adults that made decisions concerning my life. However, the silence led me to feel depressed, sad and angry. Angry with myself, for feeling this way and yet believing I must have done something wrong that caused me to be so rejected.

This thought pattern began a journey of self-hatred and unforgiveness that would mark how I engaged with others. I am happy to say I eventually found a different healing path that did work for me. More and more I discovered that I needed to have structure because this is what brought safety and predictability to my life. Thankfully, my adoptive parents were good at creating that safety for me.

## My Healing Journey

My new parents were very insightful in how they engaged with me; this helped me to figure out where to begin my healing journey. Although at the time, I did not know it as a *healing* journey, it was simply a journey to find myself.

I embarked on a pathway of seeking to understand the nature of God. My parents played a critical role in this journey and engaged me in all kinds of activities that stimulated my whole person, mentally, emotionally, spiritually, physically and socially. When I would appear upset or sad, they never asked, "What is wrong with you?" Instead, they would ask, "What is happening for you?" There is a big difference in these two questions. The first question implies something is wrong with me as a person, at the very core of who I am. The second question carries a meaning of something happening to me causing me distress. Understanding the difference between these two questions helped me to recognize that I am good and that nothing is wrong with me. My parents never pressured me to talk but they created many opportunities for me to be surrounded by positive spiritual people that supported me in my spiritual journey.

Make no mistake, this process took years, I took my time to really process, read, find myself and study the word of God. I did this at my own pace. I slowly built up the stamina to handle things. The more I searched, the deeper I went in my relationship with God and the steel doors of my heart opened as I accepted more and more of God's unfailing love. The Holy Spirit allowed me to see the pain, name it and grieve for the little girl inside that never had a voice. Gradually the shame, guilt and self-hatred fell away as the full love of God allowed healing elements to flow within me.

I found that when I allowed myself to enter into worship and into the presence of God, all emotions flowed naturally and then I would be at total peace. Next, I made it my personal journey to seek God in a more meaningful way and have a true relationship with Him, that went beyond just knowing scriptures and saying, 'I am Christian'.

Throughout my teenage years and well into my thirties, I had these powerful spiritual experiences. Each would peel off one layer of my pain, like peeling an onion. My trip to Zimbabwe in August 2009 exposed the final layer. I knew I was emotional and began unraveling towards the end of that trip. By the time we arrived back in Edmonton, Alberta, Canada; I was in a full-blown emotional crisis. On top of everything else, I discovered I was pregnant. It could have been hormones or the trip that had me all discombobulated, I wondered.

Nonetheless, all the wounds were completely exposed, and I was in need of healing.

That pregnancy was very difficult, emotionally, mentally, and spiritually. Thank God for my husband, he respected me for what I was going through and simply gave me space to do 'my thing', even when I did not understand what was happening to me, he was there for me. Often, I did not respond in a very loving and caring manner, but he never changed. He consistently remained constant and faithful in his love and support for me. It was at that point that I truly understood what my dad meant about my husband being a man of integrity in his speech at our wedding. I am grateful for my husband.

It was during this period that I grew the most in my spiritual walk. I was hungry and thirsty for God and desired to remain in His presence where I found safety, and I truly experienced the power of worship at its depth. I transitioned from experiencing peace in worship to total stillness; this allowed me to hear God's voice and His instructions clearly.

Knowing this power of worship and being in His presence shifted my mindset from pain to purpose. It does not mean I was fully healed, but I was more aware of my pain and the triggers that sent a wave of all kinds of alerts to my brain. I was more aware of what would be happening to me when all the alerts were firing, and worship helped me to self-regulate those alerts.

**Creation of Dunamis Holistic Services**

While the healing was taking place, I began the journey of desiring to teach others to move from pain to purpose. I then embraced and accepted the calling to serve God in a way that is unique to me that would touch others that are missed by the mainstream approaches to healing.

I completed my education in psychology counseling and later did training in clinical traumatology. I also took additional training in mental health and trauma informed practice. I read books, and the

Bible and I searched the scriptures to understand biblical principles, which I could apply to practical practices in healing.

Working within the social services sector supporting individuals that have experienced all types of abuse, has required me to learn how to self-regulate and remain fully grounded no matter the severity of the story or pain I hear because my own trauma could be triggered.

A weeklong training in Cross River Alberta back in 2013 affected me significantly both professionally and personally. One day while on this training, a colleague and I were talking about my passion for the work. He asked, "Carol, why do you not fully walk in your purpose, using the gifts God has given you to engage with individuals in pain? You can support them to move from pain to purpose." This question pushed me towards my purpose. Relying on the Holy Spirit while allowing myself daily moments of entering worship, because it is in that place of worship that I find peace, hear from God, and receive the courage to continue.

One of the last activities we had to do while out on this training was to go up the mountain and find something meaningful from the land, then share to the group why it was meaningful to us.

Everyone had finished sharing the significance of their items when the leader said; "Let's hold hands as we pray to end our training journey". As I closed my eyes, tears welled up, I had not intended to cry, I do not cry easily but I could feel those tears coming. Then I heard a still soft voice say, "Just let it go, it is well". I did just that and thankfully, I was holding hands with two individuals that I respected. I felt as if I was going to fall down, then as they tightened their grip, this feeling of security and peace enveloped me. I cried like I hadn't in a long time. When the prayer was finished, I heard my heart say again, "it is well." As I walked back to the cabins, my body felt relaxed and light enough to float.

The next part of my journey was to begin walking in my calling and actually living in joy, peace and fulfilling God's purpose in my life, completely trusting God with every part of my life. With the guidance of the Holy Spirit, I developed a model of approach that incorporates biblical principles to healing emotional trauma. Out of that approach, Dunamis Holistic Services was birthed. Dunamis provides support to individuals as they engage in their own healing journey. More information can be found on the website.

The training for me was about God strengthening my facilitation skills and revealing different activities to deepen conversations. I learned how to use simple things of life to deepen our walk with Christ and to heal, creating safe environments for natural healing without always engaging in quoting scripture but living out the scriptures instead.

**Serving from A Place of Overflow**

As an adult working with trauma all the time, I reflect on my own personal experiences and that helps me to move from pain to purpose and rely on God to fill my cup so I can operate from a place of overflow, regardless of what else is going on.

Over the years, I have been able to engage in discussions with myself through the guidance of the Holy Spirit and these take me to a deeper level. I have also been blessed to have a few people who have engaged with me in ways that also encourage me to go deeper. I now enjoy being with myself and am able to see all the rooms in my spiritual house. Now I can smile when I reflect on the darkest places of my life.

I have made peace with my past and am grateful for that. The person I am today is strong and grounded and completely depends on God for everything. I am no longer afraid of my past but I walk-in freedom from the hurts that deceived me to believe I was unworthy of God's great love.

I share with you in the hope that you may find your own healing after your storm. I hope that no matter how bad your storms have been, that you too can grow in your relationship with God, find your healing and His direction deep within yourself.

In my journey, I have learned three big lessons.

First, I need to embrace myself completely.

Second, I need to soak in the unfailing love of God because that love enables me to forgive others and myself.

Finally, I can then serve from a place of overflow, being healed from the inside out.

## Conclusion

God has given me the gift to be able to understand my deepest emotional pain so that I can help others to navigate their pain in a healthy effective manner. It took me quite a while to truly grasp it. I felt unworthy to be used by God. I wondered why God would choose me, a sinner, an unworthy person, an ordinary person, like me. I am not special; I am not gifted in knowing the hidden things of God. Why or how is it possible that he would choose me? I wrestled for many years before I could accept that I was a special child of God. He loves me despite my faults, and the more time I spend with Him, the more I am able to embrace and accept His unconditional love.

I am richly blessed to have amazing connections with people that fully accept me. They understand when I disengage or if I respond ineffectively and they are always willing to give me feedback without attacking me as a person and this they do with such love that it helps to build our connections. At times, we joke about my lack of emotions during a crisis, they often tease me about needing to borrow my logical brain when they are too emotional with a situation.

I own my story and walk in confidence with joy and freedom as I share my experiences. I have no fear of judgment; I have already judged myself, and I have been released from the chains of condemnation. God's love empowers me to walk fully in my calling even when others may misunderstand or criticize.

Bathed in love and forgiveness, I can work, serve, forgive and love others filled with the assurance of God's unfailing love for us all.

Carol was born and raised in Zimbabwe until moving to Dayton Ohio where she completed her high school education. She attended Belmont University for her Bachelor's degree in Psychology, Tennessee State University for her Psychology Counselling Master's program and completed Clinical Traumatology certification. She is a skilled facilitator in mental health first aid and Trauma Informed practice training. She has worked within the social services sector for over 15 years supporting individuals that have experienced psychological trauma. She worked with Catholic Social Services for over 10 years. Currently she is the Chief of Client Services with WJS Canada.

She is a woman of faith and has embraced the calling to serve in unique ways from the mainstream. It is in the past 10 years that she has actively served God by walking in her calling which is to be guided by faith to help individuals in ways that promote healing from inside out.

She is the mother of 3 beautiful children 20, 18, and 10 years old. She has been married for 23 years to an amazing husband and father of her children. She is the youngest of nine siblings and has over 26 nieces and nephews.

Connect with Carol:

Website: www.dunamisholisticservices.ca

Face Book: https://www.facebook.com/carol.siziba.31

# RISE FROM REJECTION LIKE A PHOENIX

BY NOMPUMELELO REAL KUNENE

Sometimes in life we go around complaining about everything: the weather is bad today, traffic was worse than expected, my family drives me crazy, the movie was disappointing, and you name it. There is just too much complaining around us. Though whining can be a way to build inspiration, it also keeps us from acting and provides us with excuses to procrastinate from achieving our goals. One thing I've realized is that we usually complain in the wake of a negative situation, and we focus more on the problem rather than on potential solutions. It's always much easier to complain than to find a solution, and individuals who whine on a regular basis tend to have bad health. They gripe, groan, vent, and bemoan the unfairness of it all. What they do not realize is that they are rewiring their brain. Complaining affects your brain's problem-solving abilities and other cognitive functions. Ultimately, it works against you and eventually causes one to lose hope.

We should all be more like this widow who never complained, even though she may have had every reason to, no one paid any attention.

The widow I speak of is a woman I respect, love and cherish, my mother. I will give you a little bit of background on what widowhood in Swaziland, my home country is like. As is customary in many countries, the status of widows is often ignored. It is widows and their children, particularly their daughters, who so often suffer the most discrimination, directly and indirectly, and this discrimination, results in extreme poverty, marginalisation, and exposure to emotional and sometimes physical violence. Equality between men and women is an issue in Swaziland and is still in many other countries. There is very little legislation that specifically proscribes discrimination on the basis of sex and there are also proportionally very few provisions within the law that punishes this nature of discrimination. A woman could not acquire land independently, but only through their male relatives. The purchase of Title Deed Land also constitutes a challenge for women, due to the lack of economic resources and to the requirement of her husbands' consent. You can see how everything is in favor of the men in this patriarchal society. For example, a community of property marriage implies that land cannot be registered in the wife's name but is registered only in the husband's name. The problems arise in case of divorce or widowhood, when the one who owned the title deed is gone.

My mother suffered a double loss after my father died. The assets she could have inherited were taken by her in-laws. Being widowed presents a remarkable shift, one which is entirely different from any other kind of separation a human being can experience. In an instant, my Mother lost her status, source of income, respect, (as if she had done anything wrong), and to add insult to injury, her children also were shunned. Nobody wanted to associate with her and she found herself isolated. What happened to her was what everyone else feared, and so they just stared and prayed they wouldn't become like her one day. People tend to forget that widows are humans too, and as such they need fair treatment from their immediate family members and their community as well.

As a widow, my mother instantly lost respect, her dignity, her voice and visibility, as if everything which gave her rights to be human and made her a respected woman, was attached to my father. Once he passed away, everything died with him, the love from his family, and the recognition. Strange how that happens huh? She became a misfit. Back then when a woman lost her husband; she was required to wear black, so that everyone would know that she was in mourning. It also made it obvious to everyone that she had no protector, therefore rendering her even more vulnerable. I often think back to that time when the whole community shunned her because she was wearing all black, and yet, going through all that she never complained. She fought her battles in silence and prayer. She is the one who inspired me and my sisters to be better women today. She is the woman who made us realize that we can do business at a very tender age instead of waiting for a college degree. Not even a single day did I hear her complain about what she was going through.

It was as if the whole world was watching her so that they could sabotage any move she made. You can only imagine how it must have felt to be in her shoes. I know she often wished my dad had written a will to protect her from the inhumane treatment she got from his family members. Most of the treatment was geared towards dehumanizing her, which was always a painful psychological experience that affected her throughout her life. They made it clear that they did not like her and that she was not part of the family. If she joined in on a conversation, everyone would keep quiet and one, by one they walked away leaving her by herself. Most people generally avoid talking about death, yet death is inevitable, and when it's untimely it leaves such a devastating trail behind.

The moment she married my father, her dream of practicing as a nurse was shattered. My controlling grandmother believed that a married woman was only known to produce and raise children. Giving up her career to be a wife and mother in a culture where one is not protected, was tough. Mother never thought that the life of the man who provided security and financial support to their young family would end so early. Mom had to face reality, at the most vulnerable time in her life, yet she made choices that had an enduring impact on her well-being. She decided to stay in the compound *(my father's family homestead)* through all the hardships and faced her tormentors every day. She raised my four siblings and me as a single parent with no source of income, but with faith in God that he would meet all her needs. With the strength from above, she didn't give up on her children; she never gave up even when her mother-in-law never liked her. She stood up for what she believed in.

**God Answers Prayers**.

Mother was called to train for the job that my father used to do. With training, she ended up working for the Ministry of Agriculture, now at least there was some income coming in, but it did not wash away the stigma.

When your world comes crashing down, you need to wear your scars with pride, to show how a phoenix feels when it dies inside, and trust in your capability to soar from your own collapsed ruins.

*The Phoenix is a Greek mythological bird known, hundred of years ago, to rise from its ashes after being buried, (Schultz, 2019). This immortal creature is believed to represent one's capacity for vision, rebirth and success.*

I take my inspiration from this. At one point it appeared as though there was no hope for our family, but not only did we survive, we thrived.

Remember to put your vanity aside and have the confidence that you can always find how to deal with life. Remember, the phoenix has to burn first and experience pain before it can resurrect from its ashes. No matter what kind of obstacles life is subjecting you to, arise from that disaster, tougher and more effective. Don't be afraid to fall apart; strength is built from your battles, so believe in your ability to rise and do something you couldn't have done before, because God cannot give you anything you can't handle.

My mom had enough faith to believe that one day she would see the results of her perseverance, she believed that one day like the phoenix she would rise from the ashes. She also believed she would rise through those hardships, through those challenges, and through those persecutions. Today I call her my source of courage and a walking miracle. When I think of her, I'm often reminded of the book of Hebrews 11, "Now faith is the substance of things hoped for, the evidence of things not seen. For by it we obtained a good testimony. By faith we understand that the worlds were framed by the word of God, so that the things which are seen were not made of things which are visible." Hebrews 11:1-3 (BibleGateway, 2019 NKJV)."

Complaining doesn't resolve anything whatsoever, and you will never achieve happiness. The world doesn't owe you anything really, and you must be the one responsible for making a living. Do not let your situation take away the ability to see things in a more objective manner. Be accountable for your actions and responsibilities. Complaining isn't a solution, think about the individuals who wanted to see this day, but could not make it. When you consider all the other good things going for you it is too trivial to complain about the toilet seat that men don't put down after each bathroom visit.

You can whine about the way your life is, but trust me, the world by now has enough whiners; all you need to do is act. Justifications are simply for those individuals who are reluctant to find solutions, but instead, they place blame on other people. Be the one in charge of your driver's seat, have discipline and take actions that carry you steadily forward achieving your goal. Don't live in denial, your concerns can be born without involving everyone else in your own personal life. Do not waste precious moments that could be devoted to resolving matters that are distracting you from reaching your potential goals.

My mom is the one who stood by me and supported me whenever I couldn't see a way out. She would always offer solutions to my life. She made me realize that I am capable of doing things exceedingly and abundantly well. Today I don't regret any circumstance that I went through in life, because through all those challenges, I came out even stronger and much better than before, and it's because I never lost faith.

In the West, an orphan is a child who has lost both parents, but where I come from, when a child loses a father, they are referred to as an orphan, considering the other parent is disregarded because the woman loses everything. Culturally, children belong to their father. The mother, in a way, is viewed as 'insignificant'. It is strange that the same treatment does not apply to the man when his wife dies. It is for this reason, I call myself an orphan, for being without a father. I was like a child who had 'lost both parents'. In the grand scheme of things, my dear mother was left invisible, insignificant, shamed and without a voice.

Growing up as an orphan, a young girl still has her big dreams. Back then, most young girls aspired to marry the King, (yes, in Swaziland we still have a King and he has his Queens) this is not what I dreamt about. With the support of my mom, I knew exactly what I wanted in life. I would always go confidently in the direction of my dreams regardless of the challenges my mom faced while trying to provide for our basic needs. Even though at my school, I was in fact treated differently, and didn't fit in anywhere, but I never gave up because I knew that the God that is able to do all things, will never ever give up on me and so I continued to trust in His promises. Just like that phoenix, I too had the spirit within me that I was unstoppable in the pursuit of all my dreams. Always, I reminded myself of that and would tell myself, *"I will rise above all odds and I won't give up because the God I serve is always on my side and I'll always try hard to find a way of pulling myself out of each and every situation, because the God within me Is the God of possibilities."*

Like me, I discovered that most orphans often become exposed to a host of psychological challenges as a result of their parents' death. Children who are deprived of parental care are more susceptible to psychological damage and vulnerability. Emotional and social difficulties are higher among orphans, simply because their quality of life is now different compared to the time when their parents were alive and well.

This rings true for my story. I faced many problems, including not having good friends because most of them measured life by material things, which as you might guess, I didn't have much of. As a result, they did not want to associate with me and that led to reduced social interaction, continuous anxiety, isolation and many other challenges.

Before my mom got a job, we lacked material resources, including food and clothes, and most of the time my mom would pay my school fees very late, this brought unwanted attention to me which put me in a negative spotlight. I felt embarrassed, depressed and each time school term began, I felt anxious, knowing I would be sent home to collect the school fees. I was exhausted, overwhelmed and traumatized by the status and stereotyping. As a child, I was literally fed-up of being stigmatized, ignored and excluded from activities. I felt as though I didn't belong there because most of the kids had both their parents and had all the things I couldn't afford. I told myself at a very tender age that the moment I become financially secure; I would make a difference in that community. I was determined to support those orphans who were marginalized and isolated in their communities and around the schools, and to that widow who couldn't belong anywhere in the community and whose voice had been silenced, that single parent who is raising children on their own. I vowed to support them and give them dignity.

I wanted to give hope to those in hopeless situations, to remind them that they did exist, and they still mattered, that they have a purpose to fulfill while they're still alive. I want to demonstrate the love of God to the vulnerable by giving back to my community back home and here in Canada, where I now live.

Later in life, I too got married and unfortunately that relationship didn't work well for me and I became a single mom of two amazing kids. Being a single mom has its challenges all on its own and walking this path only makes me appreciate my mother even more because the environment in which she raised us was harsh. I learned that life is a mix of the successes and failures, but I also learned to do impressive things just by following my heart and intuition. Most often, I run into God's promises in the book of Isaiah 43: 1-2 – "Don't be afraid, I've redeemed you. I've called your name. You're mine. When you're in over your head, I'll be there with you. When you're in rough waters, you will not go down. When you're between a rock and a hard place, it won't be a dead end — because I Am God, your personal God." (Holy-Bible NKJV, 2019 )

## We Can Redesign Our Future.

We shouldn't be looking at what went wrong in our lives, but we should enjoy the present and focus on what we can do better in our future. It doesn't matter what kind of circumstance you've gone through; Do not let fear control you because it will destroy you! Fear will silence all your faith and trust in God. Your situation today does not characterize your tomorrow! The life you want to live in the future can start today, be convinced that your future is bright and continue in the direction of your aspirations.

From childhood, all my experiences taught me one thing, never lose faith. I believed that one day I would pull through that situation and be successful. You know, like a phoenix that rose from its ashes.

Different things happen to all of us, and you can make decisions that will keep you in prison for the rest of your life or choose to be a pioneer of your future. It doesn't matter how many years have been wasted chasing life in the opposite direction. I knew that one day my time would come, I was not going to live somebody else's life, I was living the life that God had purposed for me. I believe in what I can do, and I choose to not focus on the mistakes I've made because those mistakes will be the ones that will pave a way for me. The only thing I can do is to learn from them and move forward in my life because I can see a brighter future ahead.

I have learned that single parenting is one task that comes with a responsibility like no other job; it's not a job for the timid. Here are a few of my take-aways:

• It's right that parenting is a ride that goes easier with two parents; it requires a lot of confidence and determination. It also helps to create one of the strongest bonds in the world.

• Though being a single mom is an uncertain and challenging job and perhaps one which has no retreat, your children will see the effort you put in, so just pull through to provide a happy life for your kids.

• Make sure your children are your priority. They will see you do great and they will also see you fail at times. This will teach them that life has got ups and downs.

• When you take up the task alone and have to play double the duties, you then realize what value you must give to your children and how precious that time with them is.

• If you are a solo parent, the duties are always bigger than your capability, but all of it will make your relationship with them stronger if done right, and you will see what an amazing job you have done.

Even though all mothers deal with a lot of different emotions such as gratitude, happiness, sadness, pride or regret, we also try very hard to divide our time to fulfill all the duties and obligations as a mother and a working woman. In fact, I am learning, as a single mom there is even more pressure because I strive to give the best to my kids, and I am also determined to show other single parents that it is possible to be a success. My whole life has changed forever. Being a single mom is a new chapter in my life but that does not imply it is the end of my ambitions. I will always look for new opportunities to give my children the best life possible.

I believe in promoting poverty relief and community empowerment to others who are impoverished in society. We need to be focused on aid so that the less privileged individuals have their basic needs met in order to improve economic opportunities for their community.

I founded the Swazi Canadian International Foundation, to stimulate world-wide awareness and avail resources on the dilemma of those trapped within a series of poverty. We need to convey confidence to the vulnerable; strive to alleviate the suffering, illiteracy, and to build a dependable network in making sure that our commitment to better life for all is achieved in a compassionate and dignified manner.

*We can make a difference in this world that we live in* by being kind to everyone we meet, for we do not know what the other person is going through. Kindness can change everything! I also want to encourage you that when something poses an obstacle in your path, see that situation as a challenge to discover your ability to press forward. Actual strength is in the hands of the one who flourishes and there is always hope for your situation. No matter what has happened in your past, I believe if you keep faith in your abilities, work hard, be determined and hold faith in God, you can accomplish all your heart's desires.

## NOMPUMELELO REAL KUNENE - CTC, SAM, TCP

Nompumelelo Real Kunene is a highly sought after, energetic, certified Les Brown International speaker. Real is also a PhD candidate, coach, mentor, and an eMCee well known for encouraging many to rise from mediocrity into greatness. Her vision is not only to motivate but also to empower audiences with a fresh perspective of inspiration they require to pursue success and drive sustainable outcomes, in a seriously funny way. Ms. Kunene's mission is to meet the needs and transform the lives of her clients and her audience. Her book "Rise to Greater Heights" has inspired and empowered many to pursue their personal and professional passion to become go-getters. Ms. Kunene's goal is to: study your current situation, identify limiting beliefs, then design a plan of inspired action to empower you to achieve specific outcomes in your life. Real Kunene wears many hats, as a CEO, Bestselling Author, Strategist, Trainer, Philanthropist, Diplomacy Protocol Officer, International Human Rights Analyst, and a Commissioner for Oaths, following her dreams gave her purpose to see her goals through and understand that she does have everything she needs to reach her full potential. Hebrews 11, Psalms 27 and 40, keeps her committed to rising to greater heights.

BOOK REAL KUNENE FOR YOUR NEXT EVENT

**Tel: +1(780) 803-5891**

**admin@risetogreaterheights.com**

www.risetogreaterheights.com

# CAN THESE BONES LIVE?

BY JACKIE MUTONI

War leaves behind a horrible trail of destruction, displacement, loss, and emotional fractures. I experienced several traumatic events during the war. Some of the tragedies include being separated from my family at the young age of six and even being struck by lightning, I thought I had seen it all. Sadly, I had not. When I was only sixteen, I was held by my kidnapper against my will for four months. I thought my ordeal had ended when the war ended but things were still going to get worse.

The three of us siblings were sent to live with our Mum's uncle who owned a farm. This was to ensure that we would have enough to eat because our parents were struggling to feed seven children living in the city. Two weeks after our arrival, the war broke out and we were trapped. There were roadblocks and many land mines that had been planted along the roads. The risk of going back to the city was far too high.

We were stuck in that village for three years. Mostly, people spent time hiding in the bush and looking for food during the night. Many houses had been burnt down by the rebels and they would hunt down humans for the entire day as if they were animals. Nighttime brought a little relief. We would come out of the bushes to look for some food and somewhere to sleep. During the entire three years, that was how we lived.

It is easy for anyone to understand how easily we became separated from our relatives among all that confusion. Our parents had no way of coming to the village to get us because everyone had been displaced. They did not even know if we were still alive, they presumed us dead because that entire village had been wiped out. We, however, were the fortunate ones to survive.

Our 71-year-old grandmother, who was in the city when the war erupted, decided to come looking for us. Everyone else had lost hope, but she said that she felt it in her spirit that her grandchildren were still alive, and she was determined to find us. It took her almost a week to get to the village, with the war slowing down; people were starting to move between villages and the city with fewer casualties. We were eventually reunited with our parents and siblings after our grandmother found us. There was a mixture of shock and jubilations; it was indeed a happy day. Later we would go to live in another village, because city life was still not manageable.

The whole region was still unstable and it took quite a while for everything to settle down and allow everyone to feel safe again. One Monday evening, I was making my way home after work. The car I was in was involved in an accident and overturned several times. It drove over a landmine, which was one of the residues of the war, the other passengers were not as lucky as I was. Once again, I was the only one who survived but received some substantial injuries. I sustained a head injury and my left leg was severely compromised, it was shattered from the hip right down to my knee. With no money for hospital admission and in severe pain, not even any medication, I could not walk, and sleep was impossible.

Some kind people, who were looking after me, carved crutches from wood so that I could support myself and walk. I was very worried that

I would lose the use of my leg. Without treatment, my leg was swollen and heavy. I struggled to carry it around and needed surgery to hold my leg in place. I had nothing to lose so decided there was a chance that I might get help with my medical bills in the city. I didn't know how I was going to achieve that because obviously, I could not work, but I believed that my life would be saved in the city. I set off on an excruciating journey and began to find my way to a neighboring country to get support in a refugee camp. I had no idea where I was going. Once again, I was fortunate when someone offered to give me a lift to the truck station. I stayed there for two days. I would beg truck drivers to take me to Uganda, but with no money, no official documents, my situation looked quite grim. One truck driver did show me empathy and hid me in his truck, and I managed to cross the border unidentified. He saved my life that day. He was very kind and did not charge me a penny.

Arriving in Uganda did not mean that my problems were over. I still did not have money to pay for hospital treatment, my leg was still painful and disabled, and the other leg was now feeling the strain. I could not even bend my injured leg and to compound the problem, it was facing the wrong way.

Eventually, and with much difficulty, I did arrive at the refugee camp. We needed to queue up for most events and needs, at times friends and other people would sympathize with me and bring me food and help me out in many ways. Admittedly, my situation was making me depressed, but I kept the faith that God would see me through.

One day I decided to go to the market, while I was there, a young man saw me, and realizing that I was struggling to stand; he took a stool from his barbershop and gave it to me. After asking me about my story, he said to me, "my sister, will you let me get you some food." He asked me where I lived, and I told him that I lived on the street at the refugee office in the city. He went on to say that "I want to help you; I see you as my sister." He got a taxi and took me to his place. He lived in a tiny room where there was just a mattress on the floor. He offered me the mattress and said that he would sleep on the floor.

The space was only 3 X 4.5 meters. There wasn't much space for two people to maneuver but that was the best place I stayed in for a very long time. At least I was safe. What he did was incredible, that day before going back to work; he made sure I had some water to drink. He looked at me and said, "We will figure it out." I was so touched, I cried when he left. For the next few hours, I managed to get some sleep. This was my first time to have a warm place to sleep. From that day forward, he became my family.

I was worried because I struggled with even basic personal care needs, I could not bend my leg, so it was impossible to use pit toilets without touching the floor. I could not manage to squat. Feeling terrible, I said to him, "look, you are young, I really need help from a woman, but he insisted saying, "right now I am all you have got, I am willing to help you. I do not want you to worry. It looks like you have been through enough already, if you don't mind, we can share the little that I have".

After work, Abu bought some cooked food from the market. He also brought back a bucket and said, "I figured this might be easier for you to use as a commode, I do not want you going to the public bathrooms, it's too messy there, and you might pick up some nasty disease. I will empty the bucket and wash it in the morning and do the same when I get home in the evening."

I was embarrassed and humbled at the same time. I felt bad that this young man was not even related to me, but he had taken up this huge responsibility of taking care of me. I was crippled by my injuries; everything was a challenge. Instead of focusing on the negative, I started to express gratitude and prayed for Abu.

Every morning before going to work, he would leave some food and water and a bucket next to the mattress, and after work, he would wash that bucket. We lived together for about a year. Once a week I would go to follow up on my case at the refugee process office. Abu made sure that I had money for transportation to and from the city. Friends would help by securing my spot in the queue, that way I did not have to stand for hours. It was as if God was just sending the right people to help and support me. There are two sides to every war, one that breeds the worst in people, and the other side, which brings out love, compassion, and Ubuntu.

(Ubuntu in Zulu **means,** "I am, because you are". Quite literally, **it translates** that a person is a person through other people. ... **Ubuntu** is that nebulous concept of common humanity, oneness: you and me both. *Definition taken from; theguardian.com*)

This young man helping me was not even from my country, but he understood where I came from and what I was going through, as did a few others who made sure I was okay. He told me that someone had helped him in his time of need, and this was his way to thank God.

I have always wondered why God spared my life through all those near-death experiences. As a speaker, I share my story and I entitled it, *"9 Lives, and Still have 8"*.

At the time of my birth, a plague was killing many infants and toddlers. At three months old, I became unwell. Many babies in our community died. Most families could not afford to send their children to the hospital because of poverty, as a result, they resorted to praying, but my mother was adamant that medical intervention was also necessary.

Our Father was against it because there was no money to pay for hospital bills, so he focused on God. Time was running out. When my mother lost her little nephew, it shook her, this was too close to home. One morning, in the early hours, she left home without telling our father and headed straight to the city hospital.

I was in a coma for four weeks. The doctors had given up on me and told my mother that it was time to switch off the life support machine. My mother pleaded with them to keep me on it for a few more days. The doctors were convinced that the machine was for someone with a fighting chance to survive. They agreed to keep me on it for 48 hours and if there was no improvement, "that's it! We switch it off", one doctor said. As far as he was concerned, the consultant had closed the case. My life was in the balance, I was officially living on borrowed time. The following day I opened my eyes. My mother was hysterical."My baby is alive!" she shouted so loud that everyone came rushing to see what was going on. She cried with relief and joy, the nurses and doctors could not believe this miracle, I had come back to life.

The second "life" showed up during the war, I was only six years old and along with my eight-year-old brother and four-year-old sister, we lived with strangers in the bush, having lost our family when everyone scattered during a shooting and bombing stint. Many of those happened during the day. One evening as we sat around a huge fire roasting corn (which was going to be our only meal for the day), the shooting started, everyone ran for cover. In the confusion and panic, I fell in the fire burning my right arm. Most of the skin came off immediately, my brother ran back, grabbed me and we ran for cover, he kept telling me not to cry and, I did not cry, in that moment. I had no time to focus on the pain; the noise of gunshots, bombs, and flames of burning houses was too overwhelming. In the days that followed, my brother would take some ashes and cover the raw flesh that had been exposed. With no medication or covering, it became a challenge to keep it clean so it could heal. Even though it happened when I was just six, sometimes I can still smell the raw wound. In time, my wound would heal. In hindsight, now that I am grown up and am a mother, it baffles me how an eight-year-old knew what to do to cure the burns on my hand.

I find it amazing that my young brother took the responsibility of looking after his two younger siblings. Whenever he ran for cover, he always grabbed our hands and ran with us. If one of us were missing, he would go searching and make sure he brought us back together. One night it was raining, and everyone ran for shelter under some trees. It was dark and I could not see my brother, so I followed other people.

There was a lot of lightning in the thunderstorm and the tree I stood under was struck down by lightning, the shock struck me as well. My brother was able to see me through the flashes of the lightning, and when he came to pick me up, I had lost consciousness. That was another brush of death. By the time this event occurred, my burnt arm had started to heal, but after I was struck, the wound was aggravated again, it is as if it came to rip my skin off. My poor brother had to nurse me all over again.

There are other serious near-death experiences but for the purpose of my message, I have only shared four. I am here and I am grateful. After three years of applications and interviews, I was granted refugee status to come to Canada.

When I arrived, I was scheduled to have surgery on my leg. The damage was so severe that they needed to operate from the hip to my knee. As a result, my left leg ended up four inches shorter than my right leg. I am so grateful that I can walk and manage to fulfill my role as a mother and mentor to young mothers. My body still aches, but I feel that God spared me and took me through this journey for a purpose. I used to experience so much pain walking in shoes recommended by the orthopedic. One day I decided to find my own solution. I bought three pairs of rubber sandals, took them to a cobbler, and asked him to add 4 inches. At first, he refused saying that he did not want to be sued and that he was not allowed to do this. I insisted until he helped me. The pain I experienced was gone. Unless I share with you, you would not know that one of my legs is shorter than the other.

I experienced the war. I saw the devastation it left behind. I am dedicated to giving women and young mothers a fighting chance in life to be able to look after their children. I founded **Dreamland Mercy**, a charity organization which provides training, education, and childcare. It is my wish to empower 5000 young women by the year 2027. This I know is my calling. This is the reason I was spared. With technology, I believe Dreamland Mercy will soon be a household name. I have walked in their shoes in one way or the other and I understand their plight. My duty is to assist them to transform their lives.

**My journey has taught me this:**

1. Forgive yourself and others, do not hold grudges because life is too short.

2. God will always bring the right people to support and help you.

3. Find your purpose and do all you can to step into it.

4. If you stopped complaining, you might just find a solution.

5. You know what you need and what is best for you, be your own advocate.

6. Go out and look for opportunities that are not available in your home.

7. No matter what you are going through, no matter how hard it is, don't give up, stay strong and hope. Good things will happen.

At that time, I had reached the end of my tether. I was in a foreign country, I had no documents, no pain medication for my injuries, no food, no home. Yet I had nothing but hope. I had stopped thinking. I just focused on repeating the same prayer because that is all I could cling to. Sure enough, God answered my prayers. He sent me a brother, Abu. I started my journey with only four tools, Prayer, Faith, Hope, and Determination. None of them needed money. If it were not for the grace of God, I would not be here today.

"I hope you will take a moment to think about how your story is preventing you from moving forward and fulfilling your purpose."

~Jackie Mutoni

Jackie Mutoni is from Rwanda, she came to Canada in 2010 as a refugee. She is a Motivational Speaker, advocate for young women and is currently writing her first book. She encountered a lot of challenges. As a girl-child, Jackie was not sent to school because she had to work to help look after the family. As a young woman during the war she experienced violence and abduction. She sustained some injuries which left her needing several operations so that she could walk again. Going through those experiences brought a lot of awareness to Jackie about the plight of women and girls.

It is where her passion comes from, as a mother, sister and mentor, Jackie is on a mission to restore dignity in women and girls through Dreamland Mercy Network. Her charity organization provides training to young mothers, those who want to go back to school are assisted to do so. Childcare is also provided to make it easier for mothers to focus on education and training. Getting young women back on their two feet is done through various sustainable projects such as making beads, sawing and small-scale farming.

Jackie enjoys singing, motivating and inspiring others.

Email: jackiemutoni@yahoo.ca

Face Book: https://www.facebook.com/jackie.mutoni

# FEET FIRST

## BY PHYLLIS KEEGAN

**Yes**, *ten toes......but sooooooo tiny. To see a couple of 1 inch feet dangling out from me was a trauma I was not expecting.*

It was February 28<sup>th</sup>, 1995 and I was 24 weeks into my second pregnancy. Up to this point, everything had gone smoothly with no complications. In fact, just the day before, I was at home relaxing with my husband Steve and our two-year old son Cameron, but things were about to change dramatically!

We had no idea that our second child was just hours away from birth, sixteen weeks ahead of her scheduled due date of June 20<sup>th</sup>. During the night I began to experience mild aching sensations and by morning they had become much stronger. I wondered if perhaps I was experiencing what was commonly referred to as Braxton Hicks, or preterm uterine contractions. Although these are commonly experienced after 20 weeks gestation, Braxton Hicks may be quite uncomfortable and sometimes difficult to distinguish from true labour contractions. Because it seemed normal, I felt no alarm and so did not mention it to

Steve before he left for work early that morning. It never occurred to me that I may be in the process of birthing my baby later that day.

I decided to call my doctor's office and was informed I should come in immediately, so I packed up diapers, a snack box and a couple of toys for Cameron. I also contacted our family homeopath to arrange to pick up remedies on the way, hoping they might help to mitigate symptoms. We previously had experienced great results with Cameron's eczema using alternative medicine rather than conventional drugs, and I trusted her. As it turned out, it was too late!

Cameron and I arrived at the doctor's around 9:30 am to discover the doctor was still away from the office attending an emergency home birth. She arrived an hour later, and Cameron and I were taken into the examination room where I explained I was experiencing contractions that had become more noticeable and more frequent during the last hour or so. I was shocked by her lack of response, especially when I mentioned a second symptom of possible labour, the loss of what is commonly referred to as a "mucus plug". This mucus acts as an important barrier to help prevent infections from traveling into the uterus and on to the baby prior to birth.

"Yeah so? yeah so?", I actually repeated my symptoms three times before she was convinced enough to have me lay down for an examination.

*"Oh shit! Oh shit! Ok, lay down.... head down, feet up!"* She knew right away; I was in full labour! Still, I remained in this tilted-back position for over three hours! She sounded callous as she said; she didn't know what the baby would look like. My imagination led me to wonder; would the baby be disfigured, have undeveloped limbs or what? I was only 24 weeks along and didn't even know how big or little the baby was going to be. I was left feeling empty and scared and she offered me no reassurance of what could or would be done, except that her office staff would try to get a hold of my husband. Not only did the doctor seem distant but the staff too appeared detached and uncaring. Meanwhile, I was left by myself in the room with my feet above my heart and my two-year old son Cameron to entertain.

Hmm… okay? I thought it was crazy that I was expected to keep him entertained while lying on the examination table, but rather than panic, I purposely made a decision to send love to my baby and transmit a calming energy to help alleviate any distress that the baby may be in. No matter what happened, I knew I could positively influence my mind.

For the next 3 ½ hours during progressive labour, I remember a nurse and my doctor both came in a couple times to check on me and offer the use of a portable phone to call Steve. Each time, there was no connection to Steve's mobile and my mom wasn't home, so I trusted that the office was trying their best to get a hold of him. I began to wonder if an ambulance might be called and what the protocol is for the safety of mother and baby.

I put my thoughts aside and focused on staying calm as I could while I radiated energy to my baby. It was a confusing and stressful time to be making decisions on my own. During this time, Cameron was an amazing little boy that adapted incredibly well and helped me to stay sane through this traumatic experience. He easily fell asleep on me while I kept my hands on my belly and focused inward with love as I continued to experience building contractions. I felt the baby move inside and respond to my love. The three of us were bonding in ways more powerful than I knew. It felt as if our hearts were beating together.

My anxiety was beginning to rise as no one in my family or Steve knew where I was, or what was going on! Unfortunately, the doctor's office had neglected to inform Steve's office that I was in full labour, would be delivering very soon and that it was an emergency! Cell reception 25 years ago was poor, and his office did not know it was urgent for him to call, so they continued to call his cell rather than the customer's house directly. Honestly, I wanted to feel Steve's loving presence, but I knew that what I really needed was an ambulance now! In consideration that I had Cameron with me, someone needed to come along with Steve.

Finally, this vital information was communicated, and Steve showed up later with his brother Bruce ready to do anything that was necessary. I do not recall my doctor or the staff helping us beyond getting into the elevator and we were on our own from there! By this time, my contractions were already just 4 minutes apart! No ambulance was called, nor was the hospital notified ahead of time to expect the arrival of an anxious husband with his wife in full labour at only 24 weeks gestation. This seemed like an absolute breach of ethics. Without the speed, safety and medical support of an ambulance, Steve did his best to get us to the hospital quickly and safely on our own. Bruce had taken Cameron with him while Steve drove to Foothills Hospital with me in the back of the company station wagon holding onto the floor plates! The pressure on Steve was incredible while I focused on our baby and me.

As a heart-felt and emotional man, Steve shares his

recollection of this traumatic experience:

*"I was doing bathroom renovations at the time with our family business, Bath Fitter. The job was 15 minutes out of town, in an area that 25 years ago had limited cellular range, making it very difficult for the company to reach me through the mobile phone. Finally, they were able to contact me through the customer's home line and tell me that my wife Phyllis was in labour. I was totally shocked by this news and left the worksite right away. Phyllis was already in intensive labour in a busy downtown area, which had almost no available parking. Our two-year old son Cameron was with Phyllis, so it was a huge help when my brother Bruce pulled up outside the doctor's office with the company station wagon ready to help. Bath Fitter tubs were quickly moved into his vehicle to make space for Phyllis to lie in the back of my station wagon and Bruce took young Cameron with him. Driving with flashers on, I'd pull up to a set of red lights, then punch through the intersection. All I wanted was to get Phyllis to the hospital as quickly as possible.*

**Arriving at the hospital at 2:30 pm I drove straight into the ambulance bay. Leaving Phyllis in the back of the car, I ran through the**

sliding doors and up to the front desk. There a couple of nurses were talking, and I tried to get their attention.

'Hello, Hello... My wife is having our baby in the back of my car!' There was no response as they continued talking, I asked again. 'Could someone help me? Please! My wife is having our baby in the back of my car!' They stared at me like I didn't know what I was talking about. Finally, they decided to come back to the car and have a look. Taking one look at Phyllis they knew what was happening and the next thing I heard, someone was shouting 'CODE BLUE!' indicating that the baby and Phyllis were in a medical emergency. Again, the words echoed throughout the hospital and in the ambulance bay, 'Code Blue, Code Blue!'

All of a sudden, what seemed to be as quick as a heartbeat, half a dozen people show up, grab Phyllis and put her in a wheelchair. It all started happening so fast. Phyllis was transferred to a stretcher and taken upstairs as I quickly tagged along. It all felt surreal as I watched the events proceed before my eyes. Suddenly, there were 12 people in the room; a premature birth of course, I will never forget how our baby girl (Marina) made her entrance out of mom... Feet First!

Oh my, she was indeed sooo incredibly tiny; only 650 grams (1 ½ pounds). I marveled how she looked to me like a barbie doll; two skinny little legs and body, Like... not even real. I thought, 'Oh My God, she's going to miscarry'. I didn't expect her to survive, but she was a fighter from the start. At only 24 weeks, barely 13 inches long, it all happened in just 14 minutes, from arrival at the hospital to her birth at 2:44 pm on February 28 [th,] 1995.

I watched intently as a team of 6 - 8 medics gathered around our baby at a little table just a few feet away. Such bright lights and people totally and incredibly focused on what needed to be done. Every one of those people knew EXACTLY what their job was; I have never witnessed such focus. And this little soul on the table, she was absolute magic!

To watch her survive and know that she was alive .... Well, I still cannot believe it because she was so, so, so, tiny.

I can't help but recall the first time Phyllis's baby doctor came to the hospital. She completely ignored me, saying 'Oh Phyllis, Oh Phyllis'. I felt so invisible! No acknowledgement at all that I was even in the room. I wonder if she was afraid, I would speak up and ask why she did not even call an ambulance for my wife and baby!

Thank goodness, our beautiful hospital system took super good care of baby and mama throughout this traumatic event. Having those memories made it all, pretty amazing!"

**To Mama's Little Peewee...**

*I knew it was vital that I maintain focus as we traveled to the hospital. Inside the ambulance bay, I heard the Code Blue call even as I entered the elevator. But it was only minutes later that I looked down to see your one-inch feet dangling out of me. You had arrived.*

*FEET FIRST!!!*

*As they took you away, I heard you cry! This was highly unusual. For at only 24 weeks, your lungs were not even supposed to start working in the womb until 32 weeks. The respiratory therapist commented a couple of days later saying, "it was remarkable what Marina had done!" Your lungs were powerful and ready to announce your arrival. You must have really wanted to let everyone know that you were here on earth to stay and you purposefully and magically engaged your lungs to have your message heard.*

*The first measures to maintain life meant that in addition to antibiotics given to all preemies, you experienced the tremendous discomfort of being **intubated**. This meant, you were attached to a specialized respirator that was necessary to force your lungs open; at an intensity that was so invasive, your chest literally jumped out. You were truly amazing!*

*I knew from the beginning that I wanted to nurse you, as this provided you with the natural immune building components of breast milk, so it was within an hour after your birth that I asked for a breast pump. In my mind, this was crucial as I could have some control and provide you with the life-giving milk that would be frozen and ready when you were able to receive it.*

*Some would have said it was impossible; certainly unlikely, and yet you did it! It was just a couple hours later we were able to see you. Oh, My God! I felt so sad for you, and for me. It was very scary as I was not sure what to expect.*

*I particularly remember during the first week of your life, the nurse was telling me you really knew what you wanted! She had discovered that when you wanted your diaper changed, you would **desat** by purposely dropping your blood oxygen levels enough to set off the alarm for her to check on you. It's as if you were saying, "Hello, hello, I need a fresh diaper over here." I found it hard to believe you were so smart. Wow, my confidence increased because I knew you took control for yourself!*

*Earlier on in the first few days, I was thankful my sister Janice had the insight to ask; "Don't you think Marina must also have some say in her own life?" It was obvious from your first breath of life you were powerful. This idea gave me tremendous relief and actually took some of the pressure off. Secondly, I decided this was an incredible opportunity to watch you grow and develop. Why not appreciate and be in AWE of what you were capable of. If you could tolerate the incredible stress you were experiencing, then why couldn't I be there for you with a sense of positive expectation and loving energy? If things didn't turn out for the best, I would deal with it at that time. In other words, for the days you were doing well, I will not worry about tomorrow! Although tears and sadness were present every day, I knew you were going to be okay. I had such a strong feeling of seeing you as a beautiful, blonde-haired three-year old, it gave me the courage to relax.*

*The following days were an emotional rollercoaster. The incredible energy requirements and stress you were exposed to cause you to lose valuable weight and drop down to just 500 grams. Remember, a pound of butter is just 450 grams. In addition to being on a respirator for the next 7 weeks, you also had blood gases being checked with a daily poke to your heel; your mouth being swabbed to check yeast levels; blood transfusions and so much more.*

Can you imagine what it would be like to breathe through a straw? *That is what it was like for Marina.*

*On March 14th, there was concern you might have an infection, as your white blood count became very high! Oh No!! Due to the serious implications this presented, a disease-specialist was brought in from the Children's Hospital to see you. Your tummy had become largely swollen and bright red. You had **cellulitis; a** potentially life-threatening bacterial infection underneath the skin, that if not treated swiftly could spread rapidly to your organs and throughout the body. You were prescribed three different antibiotics. This was a serious and intense period. Within just 18 hours, the antibiotics did their job and I was so thankful that you were okay. Whew!*

*Over the course of the next week or so, I noticed the anxiety and anger I felt were being passed on to you. It was so important for me to arrive with an energy of positive expectations; knowing that when I felt good, then you could feel good too. I decided right then, no matter what the outcome, it was my responsibility to change my attitude for the sake of you.*

*Thankfully, you recovered from the cellulitis and just in time, because, by Day 22 what soon became a growing concern, was your intravenous lines kept going interstitial, (this happens when the fluids being put into the veins leak into surrounding tissue, causing an area of swelling). Your veins were so incredibly small that it was a challenge just to get the needle in, to provide the antibiotics and vital fluids you needed. The nurses were running out of places to put an IV and not have it go interstitial again. So, it was determined that you needed surgery to have a **broviac**, or an IV catheter, placed in your upper chest for up to two months. This would replace the need to keep finding new IV sites and would provide easy, long-term access. The surgery was successful for a couple of weeks, until it was discovered that not only was the catheter damaged, but the entry site of the broviac was infected as well, so another round of antibiotics.*

*I was amazed at your tenacity to live. You inspired me! I wanted to turn fear into hope and to know with trust and faith that you too had some say in your life.*

*During these trying times, I found it to be tremendously helpful to be sure to take good care of myself. One way I did this was to hum to you when I was holding you in the incubator. This was a wonderful warm feeling for both of us. I would often picture you in my mind as a strong, healthy, and feisty 3-*

*year-old. I discovered on my drives to and from the hospital, that I could feel the release of worried tension be naturally expressed by having a good cry. This was followed by a muffin. Have a cry, have a muffin! I loved it and I was able to better appreciate that which was going well.*

*Our next challenge came in the form of immunization shots. I knew the moment you were born you would need a strong immune system. Because you were vulnerable and susceptible to all kinds of infections and diseases, we were required to wash up to our elbows every time we came to visit. The doctors wanted you to have the 3-month immunization shots that are provided to all babies.*

*"What? Are you kidding me? She is less than 2 pounds and you want to give her diseases?" I kept thinking; let's give her body a chance to catch up and grow more! They cautioned me; If you got a whooping cough, it would be serious. I questioned the fact that this decision was based on fear and resented it. I let the doctors know I would NOT make a decision coming from a basis of fear, I would do my own research and see from there. This was an extremely difficult decision, to have you immunized or not. It wasn't until a few days before you were coming home that I finally made the decision to go ahead. Along with the immunization shots, I included the benefits of homeopathic remedies followed immediately with breast milk.*

*Because I felt so strongly that breast milk would provide you with the greatest immune benefits, I was surprised when the doctor's sent you home with vitamins and iron to help your body be strong. I scoffed at this, thinking you did not need them; nonetheless, I gave them as requested. Admittedly, I was naïve.*

A year later, my brother Scott introduced me to the science of cellular nutrition and supplementation through USANA Health Sciences. This introduction triggered a stronger desire to better educate myself and provide Marina with the nutrients necessary to develop and grow a strong and healthy body for life. It was exciting to learn that our bodies produce **billions** of new cells every day! USANA has been a positive influence in our family now for over 24 years.

Today at 25 years old, Marina is a successful hair stylist. She loves to transform the way people feel and look. Steve and I are so proud of

Marina and appreciate her beautiful heart, determined mind and compassion for others. She came into this world, **Feet First,** as an example of taking charge, and has demonstrated in many ways throughout her life that initiating change rather than waiting for it is far more satisfying.

Marina, you have helped me to learn:

1. I decide what is best for me in my life
2. I create my destiny
3. I may consider the advice of others, but it is me that decides
4. To trust myself and ask for what I want or feel I need (Call an ambulance!)

Thank you, Peewee,

Love Mom

Phyllis has always seen life as an adventure. A journey to be explored and appreciated. Born in Calgary, Alberta as the youngest family member of seven, with parents that were hard working, neighbourly and "helpers-at-heart", she grew up with a compelling desire to ask questions and be an inspiration to others.

Having realized in her teens that her family doctor was focused on traditional medicine only, she began to think out-of-the-box. This led her down an unexpected path of discovery that we are the creators of our life. Her family has benefitted from the influences of reiki, shiatsu, homeopathy, nutritional supplementation and the power of thought.

Her daughter Marina's early entry into this world opened her eyes to remembering the importance of always looking *outside the box* and trusting that we are all connected. Phyllis appreciates the depth of research behind Usana Health Sciences and loves that they look beyond what is traditional and explore beyond what is expected.

Your health. Your life. Your way.

Connect with Phyllis:

Pmkeegan1@gmail.com

www.pmkeegan.usana.com

Instagram: Phyllis_keegan

# BETRAYED BY KINDNESS

## THE PRICE OF WOMANHOOD, A LABOUR OF LOVE AND LOSS.

BY ANGELA BURNHAM SPRAGG

*Throughout my life, I have suffered betrayal of love and money; one never thinks this will happen to them. After losing everything, I found myself homeless, in a toxic relationship, no social stability, and under toxic employers. I was beginning to think, this surely is a bit too much for any human to tolerate. I began to look within myself for reasons of all the wrongs I have encountered. Am I at fault? Is this my doing? Perhaps I am too kind, is it my kindness that has betrayed me?*

**How I address myself has become important to me over the years.**

I was born in Kent, England, my cultural background is Anglo-Indian, and my spiritual upbringing is Christianity. I prefer to refer to myself as an English woman because England is my birthplace, I am proud of my country and inheritance of both cultures and I love all things English, British, and Indian.

My academic history highlights how unstable my life was during the most important years of my schooling. I received my education in two countries; nursery and primary schools in North India and, high school in Southern England, at Nailsea. I completed my GCSE's, and A' Levels in Ealing and Richmond and received my BSc at the London Metropolitan University. This instability affected my life profoundly and to some degree proved a hindrance when making important decisions in my adult life. I traveled so much, learned much, seen much, and lost far too much.

**My name is Ms Angela Burnham Spragg.**

I observed women, almost in all their actions, take several considerations, often compromising their own needs and values to provide comfort and care for others. Their unconditional maternal kindness oozes forth in all their activities, which often leaves women in a complex aftermath.

Women struggle to protect female wellness, safety from abuse, unfair laws, wages, maternity challenges for career women, adopting single motherhood as a proud movement and managing marital status. Not much has significantly changed over the centuries. Where a name change is concerned, although not compulsory, it is expected that every family member will have the same surname Yet, it is always the woman, who must step back for that balance. I often wonder how nice it would be to start a new family with a new name for the new beginnings. I know of only two families who exercised this deed and it was a beautiful, balanced and kind act.

It saddens me gravely that women remain second-class citizens in many cultures, where an automated assumption is that you are either married or living with parents, but never otherwise. Women are customarily associated with their family or their children, as it is unnatural for a woman to be without. It is often difficult for many to comprehend that a woman would choose not to have children, unless the reason for not bearing children is simply that your body is not capable.

Domestic homes are ridden with instability, a third of all females are being abused and unstable family life has raised the toxicity levels against children, beyond measure. It is unfathomable to me that in the 21st Century we are still exercising prejudice against the melanin pigment found in various concentrations of the human skin, depending on the climate your ancestors lived in. Can we really claim the human race to be as intelligent as we make out? Until such a time when we can perfectly align ourselves with the mechanics of the Universe, we will remain foreigners on this planet. I strongly believe we need to focus more on family values, love and kindness.

My first experience with toxicity was also within the family home, from my stepmother. She was an evil woman who controlled my limited supply of food and even hid the sanitary towels, forcing me to use my lunch funds to buy sanitary products. My school nurse attempted to highlight the severe underweight issue, but nothing came into the light for my father or social services. She made me wear second-hand clothes, because she resented the fact that my clothes were tailor made, including my school uniform. She would take me to charity shops in England and force me to wear those clothes without first washing them. However, she only purchased new clothing for her one-year old daughter, Nadine. At sixteen, my first meeting with my biological mother was sad and disheartening. Weeks later, she expressed that she did not cope well with losing her only child, and now that I am a grown woman, she simply cannot connect. I felt kindred to her feelings as our meeting brought all her past pains to the surface and upset her so gravely that the kind thing to do was to let her be. All contact was dissolved and her phone number changed. This indicated strongly to me that we would never meet again. Living with my stepmother became so unbearable and was the solitary realization that made me miss my mother so badly. My only escape now, I felt, was to run to my father's family in India and even my father did not object to this common sense. He was all too aware of the toxicity I was facing from my stepmother. Unfortunately, my haven with my father's relatives also turned toxic after the first year.

I began feeling like the goose that had laid the golden eggs. Some family members wanted to take charge of my care because of all the financial benefits that were attached. My father was experiencing high anxiety of his own with my stepmother and I could not bring myself to share my side of this toxicity with him. My father eventually chose peaceful living rather than to save his wealth and his beautiful home, in Nailsea, England. He gave it all up and parted from his second wife and second daughter with nothing in his pocket, only his car and the clothes he wore. I shared nothing about my experiences in India, but returned to England with a heavy heart. I kept wondering, how could people be so unthoughtful and unkind? To this very day, I still ask this question.

A house of worship was the next place where I would experience toxicity on another level. Now In my early mid-teens, a family friend had invited me to visit a church, which accommodated international members. I began to attend regularly and discovered the church rules did not allow the wearing of trousers or make-up. Only modest length skirts and dresses were permitted, even sunglasses were frowned upon. These strange and ungodly rules did not serve me in any way. One day a sister of that church asked me to leave because I was in my work uniform, which was a trouser suit. The universe does work in mysterious ways but thank goodness, I was out. This however left me in a vulnerable situation at the time. In fact, the first time in my entire life, I stopped attending church for some length and not attending on Sundays was the most bizarre feeling. I am sure you can appreciate my disappointment and my lack of understanding of this action. This church stopped an individual, who was well dressed, albeit in a trouser uniform of the aviation industry, but was well covered up. What I really wanted was my own mum & dad, my own family home. This was never possible for me. In the same way, I wanted a church family I could connect with fully, that also was not possible until sometime later after years of searching. I finally re-connected myself to church life. I needed spiritual fulfillment and thankfully I found it at St. Mary's Ewell Parish, in Surrey England.

A lesson I took from this experience was that not all worship places would enhance your life. God has given you the intelligence to make your own decisions. You should choose a church or whatever guidance you need, according to your spiritual needs. What is right for you, will feel absolute and true. God does not ask you to follow other human beings, you are to be guided by the inner-divine and witness miracles taking place, and this is exactly what happened for me! I have never nor will I follow cliques or groups, and leaving that church taught me to fearlessly throw myself into any new situation and watch the magic of life unfold. This is how I live my life every day now. It no longer amazes me how God's grace guides and protects me in all my ways. I simply walk my path without fear knowing that I am protected by the Grace of God. The Divine is within and around me, so I can fear no evil.

It is wise to surround yourself with people in this life who follow the path of truthfulness, because you become like what you have surrounded yourself with. I urge you to surround yourself with truthful family, friends, and great minds; make that your most important principle. You may have fewer friends, but you will live a life without drama and anxiety.

I lost my grandmother in my late teens and had no idea of the roller-coaster ride that I was about to experience. I lived with my grandmother both in Jalandhar, India and in North Somerset, England. Rakhi Sahota was the only stable person in my life. In her later years, she suffered from severe skin allergies and loneliness. My grandmother played a vital role in building a Christian community in her town and held a respectable reputation and position. My grandparents firmly supported girls' education and made sure all their daughters were educated, in a time when this was not the norm in India. Today I honour my grandmother by supporting women's causes, education and empowerment.

The senior days of any grandmother should be joyful. Unfortunately, my poor gran suffered much. It was during the time that I was studying for my A' Levels and working full-time in a restaurant, that I also gave full-time care to my grandmother. I had always referred to gran as Dado, which is a word derived from the Indian language. Dado Ji, meaning grandmother. My Dado's typical day started with early bathing which lasted up to two hours and used copious amounts of hot water. Part of my morning ritual was to supply her with hot water once the bath tap stopped delivering. Gallons of water needed heating up daily for her two-hour bath, and I would carry the hot water from the kitchen up a flight of stairs, before gently pouring the water to the tub without scalding her. This required 10 to 15 trips up and down those stairs, all before I would get ready for college. This was indeed tiring, to this day, I do not know how I did it for three to four years! I became exhausted from all the caregiving, studying, working full-time and managing the household. I experienced no rest. This was one of my earliest sacrifices of womanhood.

My Dado Ji's loneliness is still so fresh in my mind and it hurts me even today. She did not receive the love, affections, and attention I believed she needed for her age. When I was informed by the medical staff that her end was nearing and perhaps only two to four weeks was the most she was expected to survive, I quickly put on my thinking cap. Suddenly it became clear to me that Dado Ji's entire family, her daughters, friends and all her social circle resided back in India. If her time is so short, then I must make sure she meets with her daughters before her life expires; here in England, she had only my Dad and me. With some urgency, I discussed Dado Ji's travel arrangements with my father, but he was occupied with his own battles and my urgent suggestions fell on deaf ears. Therefore, I alone saved up for her ticket and arranged for her travels. I still remember her departure; in a wheelchair, from Terminal 4 at Heathrow Airport, the light blue outfit she wore, her thick framed glasses and I cannot forget her utmost saddened and grim teary face. It was not your typical wave goodbye to a relative with a 'see you back soon' departure; no, it was a final goodbye.

In my hectic life, it did not quite sink in that I will never see my Dado Ji again. Often, I think I am still saying goodbye to her in different ways. My pain is buried deep inside me and I cannot free it. In death, we must remember what is best for the person transitioning from this living cycle. It is not what we the observers want, but what the individual who is nearing their end, may need.

My soul is content that I made every effort to do right for my grandmother. Sending her to India so that she could spend some time with her daughters, I know this was appreciated by all. Even though she had only been given a few weeks to live, I do not remember her passing or even speaking to her again. That period seems not to have registered and I try not to dwell on it, for the guilt of not being part of her final days is torturous. I miss her even today, still wishing I could have done more to make her comfortable. However, back then I was mentally and emotionally drained and so inexperienced in life and adult matters. She deserved better, but I could not do more. Even in her last days, I know that I remained her main worry.

My grandmother was a person of strength; God-fearing, patient, kind and never afraid to speak the truth. She always managed her life challenges well, so I found it strange that she was always concerned about my future life partner. Dado Ji recognized that I had a very independent and steel character from a very young age. Perhaps she had an inner wisdom that this steel confidence of mine would not be an attractive feature to my suitor and could cause me struggles within relationships because it gave me a false sense of security. She knew, I am sure, that true steel character is made, not born. In hindsight now, I understand that the steel shell I cocooned myself in was for self-preservation throughout my tender years. Nevertheless, my steel character would still face the furnace for further toughening. I am thankful that my struggles in life did not turn me into a victim, but they taught me great lessons that shaped me into the person I have become today, and I will never again fall prey to toxicity. I will not ever change who I have become, but back then, I continued with my false steel confidence, thinking that I had learned what life was all about.

One of my grandmother's strengths which I inherited was kindness, and it was about to become the mightiest lesson of my life. It broke me to the core and challenged every ounce of confidence I possessed.

My father and I did not get a chance to be close; we were both surrounded by unstable environments. We did not mind each other, there just was not much affection shared asides the daily pleasantries. I lacked a strong male role model in my life, so naturally as a young woman in my mid-twenties, I embarked on a journey with a man whom I held in high regards. He was the grandeur image of a man. The attraction between us was instant which my father also noticed and approved. His profession was in the legal sector and he was involved in my father's legal matters. Naturally, our closeness grew to a depth I had not ever encountered.

Our love was true, and we enjoyed many years of fun. We were inseparable, attached at the hip; we loved to dance, socialize and had a grand life. However, all this was not to last. Another person deep inside him began to emerge; he became a perfect Jekyll and Hyde. This is the only way I can describe him. I lived in deviant toxicity of coercive abuse for several years. Only my closest persons know what I endured. So why, you may be asking, did I *not* leave? This is the same question I would ask when I saw women enduring abuse in their domestic home life. *I thought*; perhaps because they are not strong like me, maybe they have not had an education like the one I have, could they be from a poorer background? Surely, these are reasons for enduring domestic abuse. I could not have been more wrong! I became a victim simply because *nothing* prepares you for it, it does not come with a label. When you start a relationship, it is not natural to first profile your lover, many of us place all our trust right from the start. This was a grave error on my part. I never thought about failures, arguments, deceitfulness and broken promises. Along the journey of love, your needs and compatibility do change but once the heart aches with bruised emotions are involved, the decision -making process is profoundly impacted.

My steel confidence kicked into survival mode. I began cutting people out of my life like a hot knife in butter. I became emotionless, because *the strong don't cry*. Even when I wanted to cry, I could not. My relationship with my father became so toxic during his last days that I did not even attend his funeral. I was heartless and this is what I perceived was steel confidence. This grand man entered my life and was the first person who managed to touch and caress my soul in such a way that I became putty in his hands. Everything about him was beautiful and proper, how you think a man should behave. The perfect man!

Before I could recognize it, my wide social circle became non-existent. I found myself eating double portions, completely opposite to my life as a teen. I could not be even 10 minutes late; every part of my life was controlled by this man. This is not something I noticed early because when living a busy scheduled life; you do not take the time to notice subtle changes. I endured this for so many years and justified it with many different reasons. The result was, I had fallen prey to the very toxic domestic coercive abuse that I believed could never happen to me. I didn't even see it coming.

Once I started to reflect and observe my life, I no longer recognised myself. The fear of losing myself now became the drive and the reason for my U-turn.

Leaving was hard; I struggled to detach, the emotional attachment ran too deep to detangle and I needed to set myself a plan and conquer this in stages. This perfect man was part of most of my adult life, he was a part of everything I achieved and did. I began to lay out bound-aries for everything I found offensive, if these boundaries were crossed, that part was to be cut-off from my life. One important area was my finances; I separated from all our joint accounts; I could not risk it any further. At first, I did not realize his dependency on alcohol and careless spending but found my money was either lost from mishandling or simply forgotten about. During our last holiday he verbally abused the taxi-driver to such an extent, that both the taxi-driver and I felt empathetic towards each other rather than the pain and abuse he was dishing out. We never holidayed again after this episode. I was his trophy-wife and as long as he had me, he was not bothered about the numerous friends he had lost. I stopped going out anywhere with him and we were officially a cohabiting couple only. I became his last friend to leave. He was lonesome and that was very sad to witness. I eventually was able to build and reconnect with the people I loved and cared about.

Slowly but surely, every boundary was breached. This last one however, led me to leave my home for good.

Physical abuse was something I could never accept. One day, during an online-teaching class of mine, he violently interrupted in one of his most heavily drunkard states. My fear was that he would fall in the staircase and I would end up in prison. He took a golf club to hit me and we struggled. I endured his stumbling attack on me and kept him from falling. With my body still pumping adrenaline, I frantically and shakily left the house in my car; I drove far away, called the police and never looked back. By setting up my boundaries, I gained the confidence to leave, without them I believe my future was in grave danger.

Healing will happen when you accept your circumstances and begin to pull yourself from it. Domestic abuse is a battle you must fight from within yourself. It distorts you in every way possible, but you must remember you are not at fault.

Forgive yourself, re-connect with the inner you and your values, then begin to physically remove yourself from the toxic life both physically and emotionally. Recovery will take time, there is no quick solution, it is a test of your inner strength.

By the grace of Almighty God, I conquered, and I am blessed. Amen! Lessons learnt and letting go, I believe would have made my Dado Ji proud. Even today, I adore her for her wisdom.

Ms. Angela Burnham Spragg is a Women Empowerment and Toxicity Coach. As CEO of Advantage Women Network (AWN) Company, her focus is to empower womenfolk and help them manage and deal with toxicity they may face at their domestic homes and otherwise. Women are prone to becoming financially dependent at different stages in their lives, especially during childbearing and retirement. AWN offers several collaborative coaching programs to help women become successful business owners and stay financially independent. Angela particularly focuses on setting long-term goals through strategic planning. AWN focus on the following objectives:

- Listen, educate and offer confidential advice

- Strategic goal setting, planning and implementation

- Training and skill development

- Pathway to a healthier future

- Inspire and connect with a trusted network

Angela's background comprises Aviation and Surface Transport. She has achieved BSc (Hons) in Airline, Airport and Aviation Management discipline with the Dean's Award. She is an International bestselling author, an influencer and a connector. Her long-term vision is to assist billions of women to achieve financial freedom and to stop all levels of toxicity against women and girls.

Connect with Angela:

https://www.facebook.com/angela.b.spragg/

www.advantagewomennetwork.com

# SOMEBODY'S SON

BY FARAI RUKUNDA

**Introduction**

Love is a word that is often used loosely but encompasses a wide range of strong and positive emotional and mental states. Love is profoundly tender, a passionate affection for another person, a feeling of warm personal attachment or deep caring as for a parent, child, or friend. We have all experienced different types of love. These experiences contributed to our personality outcome as individuals.

In this chapter, I would like to share some of my early experiences from childhood and detail how they have transformed me into the person I am today. Even though I have experienced many types of LOVE, in this chapter I will focus on *Conditional* love.

Conditional love is a love that is not given freely; it is an affection that is rewarded only when certain requirements are fulfilled. It is during our childhood that we first experience love. Through our parents or guardians, a model of love is created for us. Conditional love can be associated with abandonment as well.

It has often been said that people will not remember what you said but will remember how you made them feel. This chapter is written based on my feelings, not necessarily facts. Mine has been a journey full of different seasons, as I like to call them. In life, we go through different seasons, some are longer than others, but we learn from each of them. It is my hope that this chapter will give you an opportunity to reflect on your own life.

What kind of seasons did you experience and what have you learned from them?

**When life hits like a hurricane**

On March 24th, 1976, Life changed abruptly for my family. My parents, Lovemore and Mary Rukunda, were killed instantly in a car accident. Many people came from different parts of the country to mourn their death and shortly after their funeral, my siblings (Rhoda 19, Tsitsi 16, Winnie 8, and Carol 4) and I, (just 6 years of age) began adjusting to a new normal life without our parents.

It was also a new normal for my aunt Mhai, who had been given the task to be our legal guardian. I remember my sister Tsitsi, taking my two sisters, Winnie, Carol and me aside, telling us that going forward Aunt Mhai will be our mother and we needed to start calling her mom. At the time, my sister Tsitsi was in boarding school at Hartzell High school and my sister Rhoda, would also be living with us as she was finishing up a course at the community college in Harare, the capital city of Zimbabwe.

In my young mind, the new living arrangements outlined by sister Tsitsi were very confusing and very hard for me to comprehend. I did not know how else to move forward. I had a mother for the past six years who was kind, caring, and provided steadfast love, but suddenly she did not physically exist anymore. As for my father, I always remembered him for spending time with me, mostly riding on his scooter which was his means of transportation to work. Overall, I felt love and security. For many years after their deaths, I had often questioned, "What if they were here?" Then reality kicked in that they were not, leaving me unsure of the future, and craving their love and security. I needed someone to assure me that everything was going to be okay. There was so much confusion in my young mind, and I did not know how to sort out the mess.

I don't quite remember details of the rest of the year of 1976. I felt that my aunt Mhai, was trying her best in her new role as mother to five children, plus her daughter Kundi, who was the same age as my sister Winnie. Before long, I started my first grade (January 1977) at Rukudzo Primary School, a local school within walking distance from my home. That same year, our sister Rhoda departed for the United States where she reunited with old friends, Norman and Winnie Thomas for further college education. Two years later, in 1979, our sister Tsitsi followed Rhoda to the United States to further her education as well.

Norman and Winnie Thomas, back in the late 60s, were best friends with my parents and United Methodist Missionaries at Arnoldine Mission, my home village. During those years, Norman and Winnie's relationship with my parents blossomed and us children felt as if we had two sets of parents. Even though they eventually returned to their home country in the U.S.A., the bonds remained strong.

The first 7 years of my elemental (primary) education went well. During those years, my aunt always made sure that we went back to Arnoldine, my home village, to spend time with our grandparents, and we would help work in the cornfields and herding cattle. The end of the 7th year, (1983) students were required to take national examinations in Math, English and Shona (my native language). Back then, in order to be accepted into a good secondary school, you were required to do well on those national examinations. I passed my examinations with flying-colors and was fortunate to receive a scholarship to go to Hartzell High School, one of the few prestigious, private boarding schools in the country. I was very glad to attend school there and to be a part of it. The school was located 200 miles away from my home, near the city of Mutare and had very high expectations of excellence in education and ethics.

## A Sense of Belonging

My years in high school proved life changing for me. I recall the times leading up to my very first year as I was preparing to go to Hartzell High School as a freshman. I would begin to live away from home but in a controlled environment so my aunt Mhai, took me shopping for new shoes, clothes, blankets, sheet covers, toiletries, and some non-perishable foods and drinks. She also baked a full chicken for me to take along on the first day of school, as there was no food provided. This process became routine for all the school quarters which followed. Having enough food and snacks at school was very important and was very special to any high school student. There were students who came with nothing but the basics and I was always happy to share whatever I had with others because I completely understood their situations. We all came from different backgrounds and home life.

For each school term, we would live on campus for three months, and then have one month off. At the end of each school quarter, students would pack their belongings and return to their homes. The school rented buses that arrived on campus at the crack-of-dawn and began transporting students to their various destinations. The last day of school was another very special moment when I said goodbye to my friends and looked forward to seeing the family I had missed for three months. Each student would have their end-of-quarter, report card to present to their parents or guardians. For me, presenting my report card was a moment I always anticipated. I was always in the top 10 of my class out of a total of 200 students. Coming home and seeing family was always good and reassuring. The compliments I received for my hard work were always encouraging and each time I returned with a feeling to do better.

As you can imagine, I was now a teenager. As teenagers our bodies, minds, and souls were going through transformation. I remember doing the normal mischief teenagers do when at school but in the back of my mind I always felt out of place. I reminded myself that I was an orphan and that I could not afford to be expelled. I was not sure that any of my relatives would still take me as their child if I did something bad. It was very difficult to try to fit in as a normal teen when I knew that I was an orphan and felt I needed to be on my best behavior. It was not long before my life started changing. Little did I know that I was about to enter a very stormy season.

**A stormy season brings abandonment**

Our sister Tsitsi returned from the United States to Zimbabwe at the beginning of 1983, after completing her Bachelor of Science Degree in Industrial Psychology. She landed a successful career with a steel company in a town called Redcliff, 120 miles South West of the Capital, Harare. Tsitsi got married and lived with her husband and children in Redcliff. However, she still made sure that our wellbeing was in order. I remember that many years later when I was already an adult, I asked her why she finished college that fast and why she came back to Zimbabwe? Her response was, "I had to come back to take care of you, Winnie and Carol".

At the end of my first quarter in my second year of high school, (1985) I received a message from my sister Tsitsi letting me know that after school closed for the holidays, I was not to go back to my home in Kambuzuma. Instead, I was to go and live with my other aunt, Aunt Tee who lived in the outskirts of Harare.

Aunt Tee was married to a pastor, Uncle Fred, who was well respected in the community. They had five children, three boys, two girls. Two of the boys were older than me and we all attended Hartzell high school together. The reason I could not go back to my original Kambuzuma house was that Aunt Mhai had gotten married and moved with her husband to a new home in a low-density suburb of

Harare. I was not sure what to think of the news. This came as a surprise, Aunt Mhai, (my mom) had just left us with no notice. Part of me felt like I lost my mother all over again. I felt alone and abandoned but I had no choice but to accept what had happened.

School closed and off I went to my aunt Tee's home. During that holiday, I went to visit my mom (Aunt Mhai) at her new home, and she gave me a tour of their new house and it was a very awkward feeling. Here I was as her child, or so I felt, yet I could not live with her and did not understand why. Nothing was ever really explained to us why Aunt Mhai left. Even during that visit, Aunt Mhai did not talk about it and I had the same feelings as I did back when my parents died; a sense of insecurity, abandonment and craving for love. Although I did not express those feelings at the time, it still was a deep hurt, and I was confused and did not know how to process my thoughts. Once again, my future held unsureness, but I knew I had to persevere. After a short visit, I said goodbye and left. The rest of the holiday went well, and I spent time playing with my cousins at Aunt Tee's house. My cousins and I were very close and did get into a lot of mischief.

The holiday went fast, and soon it was time to head back to school and, one of my favorite enjoyable moments, that time again to go shopping for groceries, snacks, toiletries and receiving some pocket money. I always looked forward to those shopping trips and taking a full baked chicken with me to school. I did not think otherwise about the shopping, I knew my Aunt Tee would take care of me as well as her two sons who were going back to school with me.

In preparation for our departure, Aunt Tee bought her children everything they needed to take with them to school including a full baked chicken for each one of them. However, there were no groceries for me, no food snacks and NO baked chicken! I was told my sister Tsitsi was to send me some money. I didn't understand why I received nothing to take with me to school. I surely thought I was part of the family and would receive the same treatment as my cousins but obviously, that was not how it was. I felt like an outsider. I felt abandoned all over again. I was confused. I thought I was part of the family and should be treated the same but that day it became apparent that was not the case.

When we arrived at school my sister, Tsitsi, immediately sent money for me to buy groceries, snacks and toiletries. I was very thankful for it and life moved on. I continued with my education but by now I was very sensitive and aware that I really was an orphan and that I could not count on many of my extended family to be there for me or to love me unconditionally. I kept reminding myself that I had to work hard in school because education was going to be my only saviour. I wanted to do well in my education so that I could advance my life and eventually be awarded a scholarship to come to the United States for a college education just like my sisters Rhoda and Tsitsi had done.

During the second quarter (1986), the 3rd and 5th year high school students were all suspended because we had gone on strike complaining about the conditions of the food in the dining room. By this time, my cousins had already graduated and moved on. Over 200 students were suspended that year and sent home indefinitely, and I was among that group. This meant I had to go back to my Aunt Tee and Uncle Fred and deliver the news, hopefully, I would still be allowed to stay at their home. When I arrived, the news was not received well, but at least I managed to stay. I was given chores to work in the garden each day and to take care of the sweet potato plants. It felt like I was being punished for what had happened, but I was okay with it.

One morning while I was still home on suspension, my Aunt Tee came to me just before she left for work. She told me that by the time she came back from work she would like to see me go back to my home in Kambuzuma. I was no longer welcome to stay at their house. I was only 16 years of age; I could not imagine what life was going to be like living on my own at my old house. I would have to do my own laundry, learn to cook my own food, and self-govern myself. I vaguely remember being told by Aunt Tee that I had to leave because I was a bad influence on her son.

After Aunt Tee left for work, I went to speak with Uncle Fred and let him know that I was told to leave that day. I recall my uncle's words, "Son, I am a pastor and I always preach about the need to take care of orphans and today my family is chasing an orphan out of our house". As he was telling me this, tears flowed down his cheeks. I alerted my sister Tsitsi of the new developments and without any delay; she met me at my Kambuzuma house.

Tsitsi took me grocery shopping and gave me some money for incidentals. Once she knew I was settled she went back to Redcliff, her hometown. Back then life did not seem abnormal, I thought I was surviving and doing the best I could to stay afloat. At age 16, I became an adult. I was responsible for my cooking, laundry, and my basic schedule for the day. It did not take long before my house became a place to hang out with my friends. Can you imagine at age 16 living by yourself and responsible for every decision to be made in that house? Today I have a son, Tafara, who is seventeen years old. If I were to compare our two situations at similar ages, I cannot imagine how I succeeded in not getting into too much trouble and to become who I am today.

I remember one day when my neighborhood friend, Alois, introduced me to alcohol. Alois and I were the same age. He was known to be a very mischievous kid. I drank the alcohol and for the first time I felt so much at peace, or so I thought at the time.

One weekend, my sister Tsitsi came home unexpectedly during the holidays when Alois and I were drinking. I had passed out and did not remember her visit. She had come with the hope to pick me up so we could go together to visit her in-laws in the remote village of Zviyambe, seventy-five miles southeast of Harare, but she had to leave without me. On her way back to Redcliff, she stopped by the house again. By that time, I was alert but embarrassed and ashamed of myself. I do not remember exactly what she said but even though I could sense her love towards me, at the same time, she seemed very disappointed in me.

Life moved on quarter after quarter and I continued to do well in school. During the school holidays, I was coming to an empty house. There was nothing to look forward to. I would get home and put my report card on the table waiting to give it to my sister whenever she came to town. My local neighborhood friends would look forward to my arrival because my house became the hang out place. I remember before Aunt Mhai left us, I would come home looking forward to the family environment and proudly handing my report card to Aunt Mhai. I enjoyed hearing her words of encouragement because they always lifted my spirits. Unfortunately, those days were over, and I missed them dearly, but I had to accept where I was at, and continue to be thankful for my sister Tsitsi, who always had our back.

Through the grace of God, I managed to graduate from high school, and I was very proud of my work. With flying colors, I passed all nine exams that I had registered for. Back then, it had been many years since any one of my cousins from other families (other than Aunt Tee's boys) had graduated from high school. Graduating from high school was a big deal. That meant moving on to the next level of educational paths depending on your results. My success was a shock to many of my relatives and to my neighbors in the community who had witnessed my last two years of high school. In their eyes, I was an abandoned child living on my own with minimum guidance. Passing at the top 5% of my class was not what they expected.

**Time for Reflection**

**The stormy season passed, and one remembers one's perseverance....**

After high school, it did not take long before my sister Carol and I were told that we were moving to the United States to further our education. Our sister Winnie had already moved there one year prior to our departure in August of 1988, leaving behind her daughter, Nyasha, who was two years old at the time.

I remember that Winnie Thomas, whom I also called "Mom", traveled from the USA to Zimbabwe to help us prepare for the big transition. It was a great feeling and I could not believe it was really happening. My two siblings, Winnie and Carol, and I went through what seemed to be stormy seasons in Zimbabwe, but Winnie Thomas's arrival sure brought some sunshine.

It has been thirty-one years since Carol, Winnie, Nyasha and I migrated to the United States. My sister Winnie is self-employed and lives in Edmonton, Canada, with her daughter, Nyasha, and her two teenage granddaughters. Carol, who achieved her M.S. degree in Psychology, works as a clinical psychologist. Carol, lives in Edmonton Canada with her husband and three children. I live in Stevensville Michigan, having achieved my M.S. degree in biochemistry. Now I manage a group of engineers for a laboratory equipment manufacturing company. My wife, Tendi and I have six children, five boys and a girl (Tendai 29, Taurai 25, Tatenda 21, Tadiwanashe 20, Tafara 17 and Tafadzwa 7, the only girl). Our oldest sister, Rhoda, is married and lives in Sharon, Massachusetts. Their four children have graduated from college and are out of the house. Unfortunately, our sister Tsitsi, who had migrated back to the states with her family and lived in New Hampshire passed away in 2003 and her husband had passed 6 years prior. They left behind four children, three of whom are currently living in Portland Oregon.

**Being true to yourself is being willing to be humbled.**

God will often allow us to go through seasons where we feel mistreated, wronged, abandoned, or judged. It can hurt and sting, but even though sometimes you may feel abandoned, God is always with you. There were many moments in my life where I had gone through multiple seasons of darkness, when I thought I was alone but today as I reflect, I know God has been with me all the way.

I would like you to ask yourself; in what areas of your life do you feel you need to be humbled.

**Be willing to work hard.**

Success never comes easy. Every successful person you have met has made intentional decisions that lead to bigger and better things in their lives. Nothing in life is free; you must trust in God and be willing to do your part. God helps those who help themselves.

In my life, I have experienced many obstacles at different levels but through perseverance, hope and with God I managed to get through it all. I am thankful to those who have loved me unconditionally and were willing to be my cheerleaders in life.

You as the reader, take a moment to ponder on the following question.

*In what areas of your life do you need to work hard?*

**Try to live a purpose driven life.**

Many times, in life we become complacent and get comfortable in our own environments. If you are a person who went through seasons of darkness and finally saw the light, you may tend to forget the past life experiences that molded your character.

My life has not exactly been straightforward. There were obstacles along the way. It took me forty-four years before I started questioning myself why I existed on earth. It took a trip to Zimbabwe, my home country where I visited my home village. There I recalled some of the hardships I had experienced. There I saw some of my friends and relatives in the Arnoldine community who were still underprivileged. That reminded me of God's grace. It was at that moment when I started asking myself: have I been practicing self-giving love, putting others first, and helping those in need?

*I will hand over the same question to you. God gave each one of us different talents. What are your talents and what are you doing with them, what is your purpose in life?*

## The Power of Forgiveness

*"We cannot change the past, but we can change our attitude toward it. Uproot guilt and plant forgiveness. Tear out arrogance and seed humility. Exchange love for hate - thereby, making the present comfortable and the future promising".* **Maya Angelo.**

*"We who have received the freedom of forgiveness have the power to set one another free. This is a power of forgiveness that truly sets the captive free and can affect the whole world".* **Debbie Przybylski**

Once I was settled in the United States, I thought life was good. In 1991 I got married to my wife Tendi. I was only 21, a junior in college and Tendi was 19 years old. Yes, we were young. That same year, we were blessed with our son Tendai. The first 10 years of our 29-year marriage had its own challenges. I was trying to be a father, a husband, and student and manage our relationship. As you can imagine when two people get married to each other they each bring their own baggage which gets combined into one, carrying that combined baggage as a couple can be challenging and that was the case for us. To be a better couple my wife and I went through counseling for a longtime. Individually, I went through counseling for five years. During those years of counseling my therapist suggested that I take a trip to Zimbabwe, Africa, and meet all the people who I felt left some scars of trauma in my life and forgive them and let go. The requirement was not to verbally express my feelings but to meet them and tell myself to forgive them and let go.

I made that trip to Zimbabwe and remember visiting my Aunt Tee. She was very happy to see me. During my visit, she commented that I was very blessed to be able to travel in and out of the United States because not many people had that opportunity. At the end of my visit, she prayed and began her prayer with, "God forgive us for history", when I heard it, I knew she was apologizing.

I forgave my Aunt Tee, my Aunt Mhai and many others I have not mentioned in this story. I truly let it go and I set myself free from captivity. Today I have so much love for my Aunts and I am thankful to them for having been a part of my life.

I will close with one last question for you. Do you have anyone in your life that you feel has hurt you? Are you carrying resentment and anger towards someone? If so, what are you going to do about it to set yourself free?

*Peace be with you!*

Farai Rukunda is the founder and visionary of Living Beyond Hope. A native of Zimbabwe, Africa. Farai migrated to the United States in 1988 to further his education, obtaining a Master of Science in Biochemistry and a Bachelor of Science in Biology/Chemistry from Wright State University. After working at Write State University as Senior Research Scientist in the Department of Chemistry for 15 years, he moved to Southwestern, Michigan in 2007 to work for LECO Corporation, a global manufacturer of laboratory equipment. In his current role, Farai oversees a group of Technical and Field service engineers for the Separation Science product line, supporting customers throughout the United States.

Farai is also a member of the Stevensville United Methodist Church where he serves in the role of Staff Parish Relations Committee. Farai also serves as the president of the Benton Harbor Sunrise Rotary club, in Benton Harbor Michigan

**Connect with Farai:**

Website: www.Livingbeyondh.com

Email: livingbeyondh@gmail.com

LinkedIn: http://bit.ly/2DZYYk4

# A STOLEN CHILDHOOD

## THE THINGS WE TAKE FOR GRANTED

### BY MONICA KUNZEKWEGUTA

Almost 30 years later, I still feel challenged by this. If I could go back to those times, perhaps I would have been tougher, perhaps I could have made a change, perhaps I would have challenged my colleagues, perhaps I would have been a whistleblower. I do know one thing for sure; things would be different if I were given the same opportunity again. All these unresolved questions make me wonder why we treat other human beings whose experiences were marred by the wrong type of training so harshly. I believe once we get to know their story and its origin, our approach would be different.

It has been a very long time, but I am still haunted by what I witnessed. So, I ask, whose responsibility is it? Is it the government, society, or individuals? We say I am my sisters' keeper, or I am my brother's keeper. Who are Michael and David's keepers? You will soon be introduced to Michael and David as the story progresses.

It is 1994; I am 23 years old, fresh from Zimbabwe trying to navigate my way through my new home, United Kingdom. I went for my first shift at a children's home in Chelmsford Essex. In my mind, that was going to be a walk in the park. I thought, this is going to be so much fun spending time with the kids. I had no idea that the children I would be working with carried heavy psychological loads, the sort of baggage I had no idea existed.

I confidently went to the office to report for duty. My shift started at 2 pm and ended at 10 pm. When I arrived, all the kids were at school. The house was quiet at3:30 pm when the staff members who had gone to pick up the kids came back. In no time at all, the seven kids ranging from 8 to 13 years of age were in the house, some rushing up and down the stairs and others were playing some board games. It was a mixture of chaos and order, but it was ok.

I suspect the manager sassed it out that I had no experience in the area. Instead of sending me home she decided to give me a chance. When she asked me if I had experience of working with children before, I had said yes. She didn't inquire any further. I thought what could be so difficult. I babysat my cousins, nieces, brothers and sisters, that was easy. All I needed to do was to exercise love and patience, even though those were good components, they were not by any means enough. As I was being shown around, I noticed that in the ten-bed roomed house there was a room which was stripped bare, no furniture, curtains, blinds, even telephone cables and adapters were all pulled out. I recall saying to myself, "what a waste of space, that room could make a perfect bedroom for another child. It wasn't until I saw one child, I will call him David. He was 11 years old. He kicked off and became uncontrollable and violent. He threw things everywhere; he was beating up staff and pulled everything in his path. I quickly saw the use of that room. Four staff members managed to restrain him and put him in the empty room, left him to roll over, scream, and shout until he calmed down. One staff member went in and sat on the floor with him for a while. It was one of the moments where I realized that when I accepted the job, I had no idea what was involved. It was beyond my depth of comprehension. Not only did I lack experience, I was too emotionally fragile to work with children who were traumatized to that level. Growing up, I had my own emotional baggage, but it seemed like nothing compared to what the children in that home had individually endured.

There was one female staff member, who would shout at the children the minute she stepped in for work. "I have had enough! I have had it up to here!" she would say that while putting her hand above her head. "I can't take it anymore!" That statement was often followed by some profanity directed at the kids. It bothered me a lot. When I asked why she was angry all the time, I was told that she was going through some marital issues. I could not understand why she felt it was okay to come and use her workplace as a dumping ground for her negative emotions. Directing that anger at the children was cruel.

As part of my induction, I needed to understand every child's background and their support plans so that I would be able to implement them properly. I was horrified to learn about the physical and sexual abuse the children had been subjected to at the hands of their parents, relatives, and guardians. I struggled to imagine their future going forward. That broke my heart. On my way home, I often asked God, "nhai Mwari, ko ramangwana revana ava richamira seiko?" (God, what sort of future are these kids going to have?) With no answer in sight, I found myself overwhelmed by emotions. I would hold up until the end of my shift, then on the one and half train ride, I sobbed until I got home.

I was assigned to work with the youngest, an 8-year-old. I will call him Michael. On my first day, I read him a bedtime story. He was curious; I don't think he had ever seen a person of color before. "Can I touch your skin?" he asked. Of course, I extended the back of my hand, so that he could touch it, his face lit up and he said, "Wow! It's soooft!" Do you speak a different language, can you count in your language? He asked again. Yes, I can. Posi (1), Piri (2), Tatu(3), Ina(4)…Guni(10) "Oh wow! That's amazing!" he said with excitement. At that moment it hit me that his innocence was robbed. I finished reading him the bedtime story and left. I was devastated. After that shift, I couldn't hold it in anymore, my heart ached for Michael and the other children.

Unfortunately, that emotional roller coaster continued, my mind was constantly occupied by worry and helplessness. I wanted some reassurance that their future would be okay. I wanted to know they would be able to live "normal" lives and be productive members of society.

One day, a colleague and I heard Michael laughing hysterically, so we went to his room to investigate the situation. It turned out he was looking at page 3 of The Sun newspaper where it normally displayed a picture of a naked woman. I wondered what it was about the image that fascinated him. Considering that one of his abusers was his mother, whatever feelings those pictures invoked in him, they obviously had a negative effect. He was only a child yet was indulging in adult porn images. I was shocked and disheartened. My colleague then informed me that the storekeepers in the area had been advised by staff not to sell any newspapers to Michael. Somehow, Michael always managed to get unsuspecting customers to buy them for him and sneak the newspapers into the house. Michael now 8 years old, was exposed to sex at the age of three, by his parents, possibly earlier. If the people who brought him into this world were predators, who could possibly provide him sanctuary?

The next day before the end of my shift I was walking down the stairs, and at the bottom of the stairs stood a naked 11-year-old boy who was whining his waist asking me if I wanted some. I gasped; the shock paralyzed me. I had never seen anything of the sort, and to think that his innocence was taken away from him made me so sad.

I was depressed; at this point, I was becoming an emotional wreck. I had the sense to realize that my work environment was not good for me. I was going downhill. I decided to request a transfer to work with adults instead. I had struggled to cope with seeing the children suffering and it triggered an emotional roller coaster within me, again and again. I was struggling.

Even though I left the children's home, I always wondered about Michael, David and the other children. I prayed that the system that took them from their abusers would get them the right therapy and keep the three girls, and the four boys safe.

8 years later, I decided to take extra work to cover my living expenses. I reached out to an agency which was responsible for recruiting professionals like me to work in rehabilitation facilities. I managed to get an opportunity to work with young adults in Essex. At that facility we worked with sex offenders. By that time, I had gained a lot of experience and training in various sectors in the Care field. One day, while in a meeting, we were informed that in a few days a new client would be coming to occupy the vacant room.

When this young man arrived, I was certain that I had met him before, but for the life of me, I could not remember where. It bothered me for a good two days, and then it hit me, Oh my God! I remembered...that was Michael! My heart broke all over again. I kept thinking; how did he get here? He **never** was rehabilitated or received therapy; how did he end up in a sex offenders' unit? To compound his predicament, at sixteen he had not gained a single life skill. I had that conversation with God again, "when I was asking about the sort of future the kids would have; I didn't expect to get the answer in my lifetime, not that way anyway." When I worked in the children's home 8 years earlier, I didn't even know that such a place existed where they looked after young adult sex offenders. God gave me pretty much a picture of the kind of future Michael and the other boys were going to have. I could not believe that he fell through the cracks. **What happened?** At this point, he was getting ready to move into the community and live by himself.

Watching him go about his daily business, I realized how everything was stacked against him and had been since birth. Both parents molested him. At three he was taken by social services for his safety and now here we were; he was a sex offender soon to be released into the community that he did not know how to navigate. In the unit, he did everything with a staff member present, shopping, going to the cinema, socializing with roommates, the only time he was by himself was in his bedroom.

We often sat in the lounge with the boys monitoring their behavior while they watched Tv. If they looked at each other, we were required to quickly shout, 'no staring' and quickly disrupt the eye contact. The boys would have to avoid turning to look at whomever they were talking to. Have you ever been in a situation where you feel uncomfortable, but you say nothing? To me this was one such situation. It was so wrong, given that we all acknowledge each other through eye contact. Even though I covered two shifts per week, they were the least enjoyable moments of my week. I feel sad that I did not say or do anything.

Outside, the community was already hostile, for people like Michael understandably so. Parents had demanded that they had a right to know whenever a sex offender moved onto their street. I had seen on the news how people attacked the homes where sex offenders lived. I looked at Michael and saw how society had not afforded him any chance nor any of the privileges that we all enjoyed and took for granted. As if all that was not enough, the sex offenders' unit had two main policies which I felt were inhumane. The first one was the no touch policy, so even if the boys extended their hand to greet you, they were reminded to "not touch", neither could they shake each other's hands. Secondly, was the no look/stare policy. I may be forgiven for not understanding the purpose of these two policies, but I am sure you too wouldn't.

It is well known that one of the most important human heritages is the need for physical touch. Physical touch is the foundational element of human development and culture. As I write this, it is the year 2021, the whole world has experienced restrictions that were applied because of a pandemic outbreak. While this was never experienced before at this magnitude, most of us struggle from the effect of isolation. The suicide rate among young people has increased. Maybe you can understand or put yourself in the shoes of Michael and the other young men in that unit. To them, that was a way of life.

Have you ever thought, what would your life be like if you had been limited when it came to the benefits of touch? Do you think you would trust people if you were never allowed to touch anyone? Do you think you would have enough empathy to understand a situation if you were never allowed to touch, and then when someone did touch you, what would that do to your anxiety and stress level?

I would like you to pause here for a minute and list five benefits of touch. I have given you the sixth benefit.

1................................................................................

2................................................................................

3................................................................................

4................................................................................

5................................................................................

6. Touch can be soothing and increase longevity.

One Sunday morning Michael walked into the office, he extended his hand saying, "hello Monica!" because this is natural to many, I also reached out to shake his hand and the manager immediately shouted, "No touching!" I watched as his whole-body language changed, the confidence that he had when he walked into the office disappeared. I thought to myself. "imagine how hard he had worked to build his confidence to that point?" If that was prohibited, how would he and his fellow young people in the unit ever learn the difference between appropriate and inappropriate forms of touching?

Already we could see that by denying those young adults basic social-ization skills, the organization in charge of teaching them these essen-tial life skills was already exercising a form of violence. I was reminded of this when I read a book on the principles of non-violence.

In her book, Yamas and Niyamas, Deborah Adele, an author, lecturer and yogi philosophy and yoga lifestyle says; "when we are unwilling to look deeply and courageously into our own lives we can easily violate others in many subtle ways that we may not even be aware of, thinking that we are actually helping them." I believe the whole staff team at the rehabilitation center thought the "No Touch" policy was the best way to rehabilitate those five young men under their care. It seemed no one at the center focused on preparing those young men to enter the real world. According to "Yama and Niyamas", not giving anyone the tools to manage in life is also considered as an act of violence.

As mentioned earlier, "No eye contact" was another policy enforced at the rehabilitation center. Eye contact is a major component of communication, it is a type of body language, which is fundamental during a conversation. Our eyes speak more than words when we are having a conversation. Research has shown that only 7% of our communication is verbal while 93% is non-verbal. It is often said "the eyes are the windows to your soul." In most cases, this holds true. In retrospect, the "No eye contact" policy did not help Michael and his peers at the center to socially connect with others, heal, and grow? With that in mind, how much ability was afforded Michael to connect, heal, and grow?

I believe the "No eye contact" and "No touch" policies at the center were a set back to the sex offenders who were seeking rehabilitation. How could one build confidence, positively bond with others, receive reassurance or encouragement when such policies were in place.

Instead he, David and the other boys were being encouraged to avoid eye contact, which is widely known to indicate that you have got something to hide. How would you build that confidence, how would you bond with others, how would you receive reassurance or encouragement? What would your life look like if those components were restricted? Because they are given freely to us, we often take them for granted.

Amongst the five boys, Michael was the most sociable; he liked to interact with staff members and others. Despite being pushed back, he kept trying to be included. On Mother's day, he walked into the office again excited, you could see that he really wanted to be accepted, he said, "Happy Mother's Day!" to Ellaine the unit manager, to which she responded, "I am not your mother!" Once again, I witnessed Michael being crushed. He apologized and I watched him walk out looking defeated. I was left wondering if responding in a positive manner, with a simple thank you would have taken anything away from her. Ellaine's response to Michael was very heartbreaking to me. It brought back my bad childhood memories when my stepmother echoed the same words to me. That incident left me wondering, what was the purpose of having those units if they did not equip the young adults with the necessary social skills needed so they could enter the real world? We are social animals; we need to connect with others through communication, which entails touch and eye contact. We do not do very well in isolation. With these main components that make us who we are taken off the table, what chance did Michael and his fellow roommates have?

Unfortunately, I was not an expert in rehabilitating sex offenders, but I could see everything wrong with the policies in place at that rehabilitation center. Those policies only prepared them to fail or end up in trouble, knowingly or unknowingly.

Being a witness to part of Michael's journey exposed me to a different perspective, one that I think most people rarely think of. We are just presented with the words sex offender/ pedophile, which would have been the next part of Michael's journey in life at that point. Still I ask, how did he get here? This insight makes me wonder what the best way would be to support people like him before they get to that stage. The obvious ones are the things we take for granted. We get to look at each other when having a conversation; we get to gently touch each other to express our support or love.

The pandemic which started early 2020 has seen many people affected through mental breakdowns, because of isolation. The fundamental components of managing life have been prohibited and restricted. A lot was triggered, depression, stress, suicide ideation, post-traumatic stress disorder, anxiety, mistrust, and fear. The list goes on. To us this is not how we have known and experienced life. Can you imagine this having been your life from childhood? How much of life's gifts would you have missed? Ponder on that for a second.

It would appear as though I am advocating for sex offenders, but I am not, I want you to look deep to see that I am talking about a child. My whole story is about how somebody even comes to be a sex offender; we are not born this way. It is the things that happen in our lives.

Those who are first custodians, those who usher us into the world could possibly be parents or second custodians, the guardians might be the first to cause some serious harm by violating the children. Those who take over custody under the guise of rescue take further advantage of the children who are vulnerable and lack protection. In this case, Social Services violated Michael and others by not equipping them with the skills to survive. I blame society which seems oblivious that it is responsible for the wellbeing of every person who is part of it. We are collectively part of a society.

The only things these three custodians could not stop from developing were the physical features; their Social skills and intellectual skills were not enabled.

Without these and other practical skills Michael and others were subjected to the worst form of violence a human being could experience. It's like throwing someone in the middle of the sea knowing that they cannot swim.

Throwing them out to manage and function like all us who had teachers, mentors, friends, parents, guardians, and a template with instructions which society designed for us to use so that we could manage to have as much a fulfilled life as possible.

I am submitting to you the challenge to know someone's story before you judge him or her. We as a society should not relinquish our responsibilities to provide them the necessary tools early on in childhood to conform and comply with societal norms rather than just cutting off their lifeline, and tossing them out into the communities that are ill- equipped to handle their presence. I sincerely hope that the Michaels and the David(s) of this world will find a way to gradually empty all the toxins that were deposited in them at a very young age and manage to heal so that they do not perpetuate and inflict the hurt on others.

If I am forbidden to look, I truly cannot see. If I am forbidden to touch, I truly cannot feel.

Highlighted below are three main benefits of touch:

1. Touch inspires positive thinking, expands trust and compassion during interaction.
2. Reduces social anxiety and stress.
3. Boosts immune system to lower blood pressure

There are other benefits that are important to point out:

- Touch can be soothing and increase longevity
- Helps with learning
- It is human to need touch
- It eases tension
- Fosters a sense of well-being and happiness
- It is healing
- It is a form

of communication

Whereas, on the other hand, maintaining a good eye contact is a sign of:

- Respect
- Locking a glance with someone indicates that you understand
- It reveals thoughts and feelings
- It invokes empathy and bonding.
- It also projects confidence and help others build their own.
- It connects us

Monica Kunzekweguta is a Resilient Coach, author, compiler and speaker. She helps create measurable, action-able ways to enhance the lives of her clients. Monica is also co-founder of Authors Without Boundaries, a publishing company uniquely developed to encourage creative personal development, international community relations and the healing power of the written word. Born and raised in Zimbabwe, Monica spent most of her adult life living in the United Kingdom where she worked managing Supportive living homes for people struggling with mental health challenges. She has compiled several anthologies and written a solo book, Silent Strength: Gaining Resilience and Triumph Through Life's Challenges. She also works with individuals.

2020 has seen the birth of SalveTv and Salvepodcast platforms that she uses to Empower, Encourage and Inspire her audience in Shona and English.

She lives in Canada, enjoys reading, networking and walking.

Connect with Monica:

Website: https://authorswithoutboundaries.net

Face Book: https://www.facebook.com/monica.kunzekweguta/

Facebook page: https://www.facebook.com/talkshowtv.channel

# SIT WITH IT

BY MARCELA KYNGESBURYE

*IT can be a powerful word. Your IT is quite possibly the place where you do not want to go. What are you avoiding? What are you not willing to talk about?*

*IT can damage you. IT can stop you from living at your full potential. IT can take you into depression. But, if you allow yourself, IT can become your healing and can transform lessons into blessings.*

*I can talk about my IT now because I understand, I have recognized what it feels like, how it can consume you and that you must forgive yourself for allowing IT to steal your joy.*

*Have you ever dwelled in the pain and discomfort of not having solutions to your problems? Have you ever felt the need to control everything around you?*

*When you do this, you keep the pattern of dysfunction cycling because you simply do not want to let go of the control and power you think you have.*

*I invite you to give yourself a moment to reflect and recognize any changes within your body as you hear the words, 'SIT with IT'.*

*As you give yourself this time, take a deep breath, check for any sensations on the body, maybe an emotion, a memory is triggered, maybe you went into deep thoughts, a reaction, a tensed muscle?*

*You may be asking yourself, why begin like this?*

*We need to bring our attention to the many phrases that we hear and the ones that live deep within us. Often, they become limiting beliefs of our subconscious mind.*

*Have you let them influence the way you show up? What kind of impact are they having in your daily life choices? Those ever-present beliefs or judgments along with their subconscious nature, appear without filter and never come to comfort us or create ease.*

This is what happened to me.

I lived in the shadows and in fear of my IT! Unwilling to face It or talk about It, I allowed IT to stop me from walking in my power towards my full potential.

Today, thanks to the practice I have of awareness, I am able to recognize more easily when these limiting beliefs come up. Gifting me every time the choice to either stay with them, embrace them or let them go, taking a moment to pull me away from the automatic responses. Changing the normal from being wiped away by an unseen wave in an instant, to riding the wave from a place of choice, which has become ever more familiar.

I still clearly remember what my Modern Mythology Professor used to say, "Reality Beats Fiction", back then I did not understand.

From across the room I could hear the persistent annoying ring of my phone.

A call was coming in from someone I had not heard from in years. Many questions began to flood my thoughts, "Why would she be calling me?" Although I was curious, I had a feeling as if I don't even want to answer this call. What is wrong? What I can tell you is this; there was a sensation present in my body that intuitively was shouting within me. An imminent awareness telling me to prepare myself; that something BIG was about to hit. There I was, already bracing for the wave to crash. All those feelings were present in a very subtle, subconscious, yet tangible way.

The result of that call was indeed just as shocking as I had perceived. A deep profound loss had just occurred. One that would leave an emptiness in my whole being. As I was about to learn more of this traumatic event, anxiety caught hold of my whole body and I was immediately overcome with grief and anguish. What I should have done was to embrace this news and allow myself to SIT with the profound feelings of loss and sadness.

Sadly, that is not what I did.

Have you ever had a friend that even though time passed, once you reconnected, it seemed as if time had never really gone by and your relationship moved forward seamlessly?

This was how I felt about my friend Emma.

We met in college and quickly created a friendship that was based on profound respect and understanding of each other's path. We went through a lot together, supporting each other through life's transitions, holding hands through pleasant and unpleasant times.

I really do not remember how long it had been since our last call but even when it felt like forever, we were ready to pick up from where we had left off and continue filling each other in with all our daily life events.

At this point in our lives however, we were living a far distance from each other, and the experiences we were having felt equally distant, but through the magic of video calling, we kept our friendship and shared our whereabouts and life adventures. Sometimes from a restaurant, a park, or from the comfort of our kitchen table while we were in our jammies, we would check in on each other often and always enjoyed all our times together, from silly conversations to sacred ones. We had so much fun and our visits brought back to life priceless memories, along with feelings of well-being and care for one another.

Suddenly and without any warning, all that was abruptly stopped. One day while I was away from home attending an energy-healing workshop, I recall having two unique experiences. The first; I felt the passing of a family member to a terminal illness. The second was an unrecognizable strike straight to my heart.

Later that day, I received a message from Emma. It was kind of an encoded message, confusing to say the least, but in hindsight now, I know it was a disguised shout for help. I sent a text right back, but never received an answer. I decided to travel back home and call her once I had arrived. It was Sunday night, and Emma answered in a whisper, "I can't really talk now", she said, "my husband is asleep right next to me". That was our last interaction. The last time I would hear her voice.

It was already Wednesday, I still had not been able to touch base with Emma and although my mind was still wondering why and what the text could have meant, I had to let it go, hoping things were just a little unsettled.

Unfortunately, that was far from the truth. I had ignored my gut feelings! Now, I am learning that Emma is gone, and had in fact, passed away on Monday.

This news took me into a tight and dark mental labyrinth, many pathways in and yet no way out. Overwhelming confusion consumed me as I began to witness this event through the news. Photos with police tape around her house! My mind exploded as I tried to make sense of it all and I heard them tell that an investigation was taking place.

Not knowing the details of what had occurred, I was so far away, yet even the fear of retaliation had gripped my mind. I went deep into my memories, searching for every piece of information that could give me a hint into what may have happened. I began recalling all our conversations, I went through her Facebook profile, my mind was turning nonstop. I reached out asking for help, I wanted to know more, how to get in touch with the police department, with a detective or a lawyer. I spent night and day thinking about it. Questioning her last moves, the last words I heard, cries for help. Still, this was a violent mystery to my mind.

Not able to attend her memorial service, I slipped into a deep state of sadness and hopelessness. I simply could not understand the loss and it was far too much to bear. Not only the feelings that arose because I could no longer grab the phone and reach her, but also those of guilt, not having been able to help her, to stop the chain of events that could have changed her destiny. I felt pain in every one of my bones. The screaming within my thoughts was so loud and kept going in circles. I lost clarity and even sense of time.

Time passed as it does, and with the arrival of winter, it made my trip inward easier. I even stopped practicing self-care, all of it, gone at every level, just plummeting down the proverbial rabbit hole. I did not want to live anymore. I was like a shadow lifelessly surviving, just waking up to do what I could and going back to sleep. I kept trying to embody the pain that my friend must have gone through, I needed to understand. This was my reality created to deal with the loss. There was nothing around me to make me feel sad; it was all within. Feeling like no one cared, as if no one needed me here, feeling as though I was not contributing at all. I stopped being present and time disappeared. Guilt consumed me as I took on my friend's silence and pain. At times, I didn't even notice that the birds were singing, grief blinded all my senses, even from the warmth of their song. Life had lost its meaning, my connection to her was so strong that the only thing I wanted to do was go join her. Only a thin string was keeping me here.

*Have you ever wondered; when do we start numbing ourselves and why do we do it? How do we do it? Consciously, or subconsciously? By trying to distract ourselves from what's going on around us and from the pain it causes, we start pulling ourselves away from who we truly are. We retreat from our higher purpose and our destiny, and it stops us from facing the real question we should be asking; what is the gift that I am here to share with others?*

One day, I learned of an amazing opportunity, one that matched almost to the dot what I had been asking for. It was a chance to understand why this had happened to my friend. Although hesitant, I accepted the challenge, little did I know, this journey would not only take me on a path of learning about unhealthy relationships, domestic violence and sexual assault, but it would be the catalyst to begin my own emotional healing. I began working, as an advocate for the Rape Crisis Center and through this experience slowly was able to recognize how what had happened to Emma, matched up like a recipe for tragedy.

I worked really hard inside not to judge the event that claimed her life, her choices, my choices, our relationship, what I knew, what I didn't know, even what could have been done. Working with survivors of sexual violence was devastating to witness, yet at the same time, it opened my eyes to situations that I had never recognized for what they truly are; an unfortunately common reality to many. I learned of facts such as; 72% of all murder-suicides involve an intimate partner.

20 people per minute (10+ million per year) are physically abused by an intimate partner in the US alone, and that there are 20,000+ phone calls a day that go to domestic violence hotlines nationwide, and most importantly; how to be present for the real people behind the stories.

Through this opportunity, I was eventually able to help myself while helping others. I began to realize the services we were providing were not to the (society-labeled) victims, but to the real survivors of abuse, they were the true heroes of their situations.

Every day was different, yet every day was the same. Hearing about violence and fear, the lack of understanding and communication, unresolved problems and mindsets that needed to change. During those days, I learned to be supportive, engaged in healing conversations with a deep listening and a big open heart that allowed spaciousness. Yes, I had moments of success, peace, calm and new discoveries, but I was witnessing examples of what we really cannot see in others lives that is invisible to our eyes.

Many times, we require someone else to show us, explain to us what he or she is observing, or to invite us to be open, curious and accepting, and to simply remind us where to find our inner strength.

I can say that a miraculous transformation began within me. I found compassion for myself, for my friend, even for her perpetrator.

What I did not find was a simple fix or a one-time solution. Even when things feel somewhat stable or back to normal, life still finds a way to remind me of the inevitable presence of change. The constant; that things do not stay the same, not for good or for bad. The stories I was listening to were not cleansed away as soon as I would have liked, you cannot just wash events like these away from your mind or heart. All too often something would remind me of past events in my life and often take me into thoughts of an uncertain future, triggering feelings of insecurity and fear.

I thought I had grown strong yet little by little through my empathy for others, I had allowed the distress of others to accumulate and saturate my own emotions. Once again, I felt myself becoming frozen. Yet deep inside, I knew I could not do life as before.

*Have you ever experienced a time when you have let your guard down and something unexpected occurred?*

Once again, this kind of event tried to hijack me once more.

I awoke one morning to learn of three more friends, who passed the previous night. One was due to unanticipated health complications, but the other two; a beloved couple in the community who had become the victims of a crime.

Struck again by the unforeseen nature of these deaths, I recounted stories and they gave me flashbacks of what I had lived through when losing Emma. Feelings of regrets and frustrations that still lived in my body started to awake. All those reminiscences of how disheartened I had felt, and the avoidance I had towards grieving these losses, began to spiral my thoughts downward once again.

However, this time, I was prepared to face my IT head on.

I have learned through experiences that pain and sorrow are always present in life, hopefully just as equally as joy and love. Many things have happened in my life yet meeting death repeatedly through the loss of loved ones, have been pivotal moments for me.

*How can you go from panicked fear to fearless?*

*How can you find that catalyst within that allows you to be ready to accept transformation when opportunity lays it in your pathway?*

Later that day, I was preparing to attend an online retreat. Debating whether I should attend or not, I had thought up every possible excuse to avoid it, mostly on-account-of its virtual format.

You see, even as I write this, our world is living through a time of uncertainty and change unlike anything that my generation has ever seen before. We are experiencing a global viral outbreak, and we have policies in place to assure that everyone maintains a social distance. So, this retreat is to be held online and will be attended by each person, from his or her own home. This was something quite unimaginable for this type of an event. With so many strict enforcements surrounding face-to-face meetings, I could not imagine how this retreat could possibly be an effective therapy or learning tool within a virtual setting.

Under normal circumstances, these retreats create the perfect atmosphere for a healing practice. One which; by the weakening of the physical, mental and emotional bodies, would allow for breakthroughs in any or many aspects of life. I recognized its value. It created a sense of expansion even when things got tight. It has allowed me to experience the power of change, will forces, and the availability to be with myself, really present to myself and the world I had created around me, and to the part I play in that world. It was going to be the second retreat of this type for me, and the first one was tough enough attending in person that here I was having constant doubts about attending this event without the physical and emotional interaction of others. At a retreat of this nature, pain, suffering, vulnerability, desires, trauma, loss, really anything and everything can surface.

So, the question I really was asking myself was this;

Do I want to sit alone at home with all these feelings inside me?

Yes, all of us within the group will be grieving deep losses or issues but many of us are having doubts as to the successful outcome of such an event being held in this physically distanced format.

Well, I suppose even when it comes to matters such as these, those limiting beliefs we spoke of earlier, try their best to undermine everything we do. I am so glad I gave myself the space to breathe, to reconsider, in spite of my doubts and on top of my once again grieving heart.

Little did I know the empowerment that I was going to harvest from that experience.

I truly found the literal meaning of, 'Sitting with Grief'.

Yes, even though I was all alone at home, I was still within a group. I recognized periods in which I was being held by the others, and we had created a container. At times, I also felt the independent nature of being human. The common denominator was the intense pain that made time and life freeze. Amazing as it was, even when sharing the same space and practice, the 'results' that came out of that retreat appeared in unique ways for all.

Grief reminded me of the importance of my presence on this earth. Feeling tired as can be, yet it taught me discernment.

Meditation shouts at me, "Make each breath count!"

Many types of grief accumulate in our bodies from past failures, experiences, judgments, or anticipated expectations.

All those encapsulated joys unobserved yet, unacknowledged.

Daily, I had been sharing joy practices online, and I noticed that almost as soon as I started, friends reached out. I was having amazing conversations; we were catching up on our lives and creating new safe spaces together into which vulnerability was not only invited, but also welcomed.

A passion inside of me was reignited!

As a teacher, I was creating content, inspiring others, watching them grow and transform. It has been a priceless gift and I am grateful to have had the opportunity to witness, many times.

Not everything flows as sweet as honey. Difficult situations that need attention show up too and we allow these happenings to guide our journeys together and take us to a place of recognizable healing.

We discovered how unwilling to change we are, and we recognized how all the fears and our past events contribute to this and find common patterns in these interactions.

As we go through life, we play conversations in our heads as broken records more often than not, and they keep us stuck, trapped in a circle, going nowhere, yet we still expect different results without modifying our behaviors.

Practicing and celebrating joy, success and new beginnings is a great place to be. Specifically, after one spends years practicing disappointments, failures and abrupt endings. Even though many of us have made that new discovery of the practice of joy, we notice that what has allowed us to get there was often a deep loss of some sort. It was like learning to speak a different language, one of love, joy and compassion, and it certainly had to be fine-tuned individually. Nevertheless, we all had something in common; we had a wound in our heart that needed caring.

Today I am grateful for the joy practices, and within that shadow that was covering me, I was able to listen to a soft inner voice that shone a light. It was bringing different thoughts to my mind that steadily transformed into actions and literally brought me back to life.

With this, I found a new impulse, a motivation and desire to serve others. To accompany them through their heartbreaking experiences and utilize tools and techniques which allow their inner wisdom to shine.

*Your journey is unique and multidimensional. How would it feel to start shedding what you do not need anymore, to let go of those known habits and limiting beliefs that have been stopping you from living fully?*

Your time is now!

I hope that you will remember just one word from my story. It is easy enough to remember, but few truly understand the power it has. It unlocks infinite possibilities for You!

I like to give the word meaning in this way;

SIT: Stillness, Inquiry, Transformation.

Practice Stillness: whenever and wherever you are, pause, invite clarity, feel yourself within your body and surroundings.

Invite Inquiry: live in the question, be confident, open and receptive to the answers that may show up.

Embrace Transformation: have the certainty that everything changes, that there will be joys and sorrows and that you have the ability to transcend all of it.

Going through this process has allowed me to create the 'Experiencing Being' Program and Practices. SIT of course is now a new pearl.

There are many kinds and stages of grief, all different, yet all the same. Now I know that the difference lies in how you approach this, if you observe it or not, if you nurture it or feed it, if there is real or perceived pain.

*Are you ready to change, to make a pause, to have a real breakthrough, to say enough is enough, to tell yourself, I am here for a reason, to step into a conscious before and after in your life?*

I know this can be challenging. I know it is not easy to hear these words and act upon an offering such as, "Just Sit with It", or "Just Breathe".

Breath work has been a life changer for many others and myself, we still need to be prepared, to be patient and to practice. Yes, breathing is a natural and free gift available at all times, yet we need to learn how to use its healing properties, especially, after experiencing traumatic events.

Finding it difficult to breathe manifests too as we are living with violence around us, or the loss of a loved one. We all have had that one individual that can make a smile appear naturally on our face. One that you remember today and are grateful for their presence in your life, for having been able to share this journey on earth together and the blessing of growing together through time and space.

Perceive now the warmth of their words, the sound of their voice, their loving hugs, their support and care.

These days, I remember to breathe, to be present with my whole being! I remember that I am worth every breath. I am valuable and I deserve to be alive! I can give and receive, and I am here for a reason. There is something bigger than I that guides me and is with me and I am here to contribute on this earth; and this earth would be different if I were not here.

I have learned to recognize my own essence and connect with my presence. I have let go of all those times when I felt there was no need for me to be here, no reason to stay, no one would miss me, and then turning around and being able to see the many clues which showed me otherwise.

I knew that just existing was not a choice. This coasting through life was not enough. I was ready to surrender and listen to this new calling; I was ready to say YES! Yes, to myself, Yes to life!

I invite you to take responsibility and experience your own breakthroughs! Everybody can benefit from watching how you transform your life and start to live on your own terms, expressing your truth.

I hope I have inspired you to draft your own comeback story.

Marcela is a Transformational Coach that's passionate about using the body, emotions, thoughts, and present moment awareness, to ignite YOUR inner fire, to deeply listen to YOUR wisdom, to create spaciousness, freedom and choices that will bring JOY back into YOUR life!

As an avid learner, she has trained, studied, practiced and condensed more than 15 years of energy healing modalities. Her background as a Chemical Engineer, Waldorf Teacher, Grief Support Specialist, and more have created an interconnection & deeper understanding of energy, matter, and the power of transformation along the path of human biography.

She invests her time working with clients to discover limiting beliefs and recurring patterns. These are transformed, allowing for new mindsets to be created which will lead to achieving a lifetime of enthusiasm, ease, motivation and abundance.

She empowers teachers by sharing with them trauma informed mindfulness practices imbued with beauty, inspiration, goodness, & courage for the truth.

Born and raised in Mexico, she now resides in the U.S. She enjoys learning, being creative, weaving, playing shakuhachi, and most of all spending time with her husband & cats!

Connect with Marcela:

Website: www.marcelakyngesburye.com

Facebook Page: https://www.facebook.com/MarcelaKyngesburye

Grupo en Español: https://www.facebook.com/groups/alegriayentusiasmo

SIT WITH IT

# LIVE AND LEAVE YOUR LEGACY

BY YOLEEN NAIDOO

I am always in high spirits and enjoy every moment of my life. I always look for the positive in everything and in everyone. I thought everything was so perfect in my life. Even though I was extremely happy, for some reason I felt a small void.

I remember attending a conference and the speaker asked us to close our eyes. She then asked us the most powerful question that immediately spoke to my soul and changed my life.

"If you were to die right now, what would be your biggest regret? If you were lying in that grave could you say; you did everything you were supposed to do. Would you have any regrets? "

When I opened my eyes, a memory came to mind, I recalled hearing a preacher saying; "the grave is filled with so many dreams that have not been fulfilled." Suddenly it felt like a ray of sunshine had opened me up and was filling that void. I had my answer! I realized that although I was happy, I had not used my time properly. I still had dreams to fulfill. I had not completely lived my calling on my life. Upon arriving home, I began to write down all my dreams and all the new visions that started flooding my brain; I gave myself a time limit for each goal. I immediately started working on completing this list. I was suddenly so energized and excited and felt a full force of power go into control from inside of me and now the void that I felt had gone. At that moment I realized, if you are living your full calling on earth, you will never feel the void.

I have always tried to help people find their own rainbow, but it was the first time I started taking stock of my own life. I wanted to truly understand why I was always so happy and fulfilled. What was my foundation? Who am I?  I now wish everyone could have that same fulfilled feeling. I wanted everyone to be happy from inside out. This feeling I felt was a feeling of completeness and true happiness.

I became aware that someone or something cultivated my thought process. Why do I do what I do? Who am I? Why could I always do the impossible with ease? I soon discovered; it was the little things in my life that added to my mindset. It was the people and role models that surrounded me that had an impact on who I have become. I had a good set of strong and persevering people that I grew up amongst.

**Father's Strong Voice**

The strongest VOICE that made a difference to my mindset was my dad. He was not a man of many words but when he spoke, I believed him. His words made such a huge impact to my thoughts. It was a force I trusted; and that voice pushed me to visually see my victory. I remember one day sitting with my dad when my brother mentioned how the recession was affecting the economy and how people were suffering. My dad looked up and spoke in his kind, firm, and positive voice, "there is no recession. It's all in your mind. If you have a vision, you focus on it, work hard towards it, put God first and you will achieve it. If you worry about the things around you, you will lose focus of your vision." He used himself as an example and said, "whatever I wanted to do, I always achieved it." He said again, "Have a vision, put God first and then God will always open the way for you, and you will not fail." Immediately my mindset fixed itself on winning. When I look back, I remembered, he was never afraid of any challenge.

He would go after his vision in a very calm, empowering, upright, positive and fearless way.

My whole life, I never knew him to lose a deal in business and he was always able to solve any situation, in a crisis. I had an uncle L.P Naidoo who was a doctor and a man I admired and respected very much. One day during a conversation with my mum and I, he said; "Your father is functioning on an energy light level that very few people in life have." He continued to say, "only certain people are born with it." I knew the light energy represented my father walking in his calling in life. He owned a victorious mind for sure. Even though I am a very headstrong person, his voice could change my thoughts. I smiled to myself and thought; if my dad can get me to listen, he definitely possesses a supernatural mind, and I wanted that! I wanted to be like him. To be fearless, strong, victorious and powerful; and he didn't seem to use much energy to get things done.

One day I was sitting in front of the fireplace in our family room. It was a wonderful afternoon and my dad was speaking to us. When it was my time to talk, I looked at him and said; "Dad the only thing I want from you is your blessing to be a businessperson like you." When he looked at me, I suddenly felt I had it. In a few weeks my career did soar after that. I soon was able to close the biggest contract deals within a few minutes using a few words. It seemed as though I could easily gain the person's trust. I recall working for a company where not even the owner could do what I accomplished. One day while talking to a total stranger on the phone, the conversation went from a spiritual topic to finalizing a multimillion-dollar deal. He simply said to email him the paperwork and he would send me the cheque. It did not matter that I was a girl, a stranger he never met or knew, yet he was willing to invest in a project he never even saw.

**Mother's Prayers**

I was a very quiet child and always followed my mum wherever she went. I would constantly walk behind her and sit next to her. My mum is a very active, beautiful, happy, prayerful warrior and worked in the accounting field. She was crowned a queen at a pageant just shortly before she married my dad. I admired my mum, she is an exceptional mother, and people love her because she is a very honest woman.

Whenever my mum knew I was going through a troublesome time, she would give me a bible verse and tell me God was in control, and that she was praying for me. She is my spiritual mentor. My mum always kept the house immaculately clean, yet once a week she would do a spring-cleaning; washing carpets, curtains and cleaning the windows. When I was a little girl, I would silently follow and wait for her to ask me to help. She always took control of everything she did, and I would help by giving her the soap while she washed the curtains. I would also help her by taking the clothes out of the bucket, handing them to her as she hung them on the clothesline then I would give her the hooks to hang up the curtains and clothes. I guess that's why I am OCD (obsessive compulsive disorder) in cleanliness. She would always tell me to put God first and to always speak the truth no matter how bad the situation gets.

One day she told me a story about a mother and son. The son would always do the wrong things when he was young, and the mother would always cover up for him. One day, when he had grown up, he was sitting in the courtroom and was pronounced guilty for murder. He was sentenced to spend a lifetime in prison. He was crying and then asked to speak to his mother one more time. As she came closer, he told her he wanted to tell her something in her ear. She turned her ear to him, and he bit her ear off. He then told his mother, as he spat the ear out, 'if you had taught me the right things I would not be going to jail today'. After hearing that story, I was so terrified of lying and going to jail. My mum continued to tell me that everything starts with a lie and could eventually lead a person to murder. There is no big sin or small sin. Wrong is wrong!

**God Is My Firm Foundation**

We lived in a small town in South Africa, and I had to go to the city to study Graphic Designing. One day upon my return home, mum and I visited my aunty Vinigy. She is my mum's sister, and she bakes the best cakes for teatime. I call her my sweet tooth aunt! During that visit, she told me that a vacancy was coming up at the magistrate's office and that I should apply. I followed through on her suggestion and I was so nervous not knowing what to expect when I received the invitation to an interview. I remember making a vow to God that morning as I was driven to the interview. I promised God that if he gave me the job, I would give him my entire first month's salary. The interview went very well, and I was given the job of a typist. I really was not sure what I was doing. I was computer literate as I had studied graphic designing programs. However, the last time I used a typewriter was in standard 6. At the end of the week, my boss called me in. He apologized and said he had not followed proper protocol hence there was a need to wait for the head office's approval first before I started working. He gave me a cheque for a month's salary and said he would call me to advise on the way forward. I thought he was just being nice while he was firing me. I took my cheque, went home and stared at it. The salary cheque was really a big amount and then I remembered my vow to God. I also remembered my dad was a man who always kept his word and I believed my Heavenly Father gave me that job andI just messed it up. I still had second thoughts on how much I should give to God.

That Sunday at church when the offering bag was passed to me, I put all the money in it, every single cent. I felt good and never gave it another thought. Two or three months later, I received a phone call. To my surprise it was the magistrate who said all the paperwork had been completed and I could officially start work that Friday as Head of the Receiver of Revenue Department. I remembered my vow. I was so excited not only because of the job but because of the experience of an answered prayer! God became so real to me. He knew me by name. I must say ever since that day I have never been without a job and every time I went for an interview; I was hired on the spot. That is the power of a vow with God.

## Generational Blessings

I used to love visiting my grandmother. We lived close to her and usually on Saturdays and Sundays, everyone would gather at grandma's house. I used to call her Ava. It's a Telugu word, which was the language my grandmother spoke, and it means granny. Towards the later part of her life, Ava became a born-again Christian. She was a very strong, poised, and elegant woman. Always smartly dressed in her sari and heels with perfectly styled hair and she always had a welcoming smile.

One summer's day, I was sitting with grandma and her younger sister who we called Shuma. We were looking at her beautiful garden filled with lemon trees, ferns, flowers, and vegetables. She took so much pride in it. The two grannies were having a conversation in Telugu, of which I did not understand a word of what they were saying. I turned to my granny and asked her why she didn't teach us Telugu. Her answer was that she only spoke English at home with her children and grandchildren because with English as our first language we would be able to travel the world and work anywhere. Voila, I am writing this book from Canada! She was always such a forward thinker and a very modern lady. She would tell us to always be smartly dressed. Grandma was a dressmaker and a very good one at that. She knew the latest fashions and sewed the most beautiful dresses for us beginning with ones for our christening. She would even sew christening swings for newborn babies. She was a very fancy and positive granny who lived to almost 100 years and still had her full set of teeth including wisdom teeth.

I never heard her complain or that she ever borrowed money. She loved people and was constantly surrounded by visitors.

Every morning she would wake up at 7 am, make her bed with pillows perfectly positioned and her white bedspread also perfectly draped. I was in awe of my grandma. Even though she used a walking stick, her king-size bed and room were so clean, with everything in its perfect place and not one piece of dust. After making her bed, she would take a bath, get dressed, and then straightway go down onto her knees to pray. I thought what a powerful woman she must be. Then she would get up and make breakfast. Her favorite was homemade rusks. She would dip thickly sliced bread in milk and then bake them in the oven. They were delicious.

One beautiful warm afternoon I went to visit her. The kitchen door was open, and I saw her beautiful smile as I walked in. She was making pollies, an Indian dish that is sweet pastry filled with coconut, my favourite. I sat down and watched how she patiently made the most perfect shapes and filled it with ease. My granny loved telling us stories of her life and I was always intrigued to listen. She told me how she would bake with her dad and he would put a penny into the cake mixture before baking it. All the children would wait for a piece of cake to see who was the lucky one to find the penny. Granny told me how she would help him make biltong and add spices down to the detail. She also told me she had her parents and parent-in-laws' blessings over her life. She said not one day did she ever tell them a harsh word and was always there when they needed her. She said before they died; they gave her their blessings.

In 2003, I moved to Canada and a few years later my granny flew 22 hours, transferred between three planes from South Africa to Canada to visit us. She said she had prayed to God to visit Canada before her death. She traveled together with my two aunts and my uncle. We were sitting in our TV lounge, overlooking the lake and having tea. I was so amazed, Granny looked refreshed and happy as she was telling us stories of her life while my aunts and uncle were exhausted and sleeping. Here, this woman, almost 100 years of age, looked as if she was not tired from the long journey! I thought she was definitely a blessed woman. She told me how she handled her finances, prayed and trusted God for everything in her life, and how good God is. Granny said the power of blessings will carry us through life, keep us safe and happy. I looked at her and realized that indeed she was a fully blessed woman, then I turned to her and said, "Ava before you die, all I ask for is your blessing and to know how to handle money." She immediately said, "you can have it now." Taking both my hands, she held them together and declared, "all my blessings I give to you" then she rubbed her hands onto mine, looked up at me and said again, "All my blessings are yours!"

**Light the Fire**

It was a cold day; I awoke, had a shower, and also showered my daughter, who was nearly two years old. It was my best part of the day, dressing her up and making her look like a princess, I loved this. She was always happy, full of smiles and energy. I called her my 'bundle of joy'. She would look at me so trusting, just waiting for me to surprise her with an outfit each morning, then she would sit on my lap and wait for me to make a pretty hairstyle on her. After getting dressed, we would have breakfast and I would read stories to her. She loved stories.

The phone rang, it was her father, my soon to be ex-husband. He told me his lawyer had contacted him advising that he needs to pay child maintenance. He asked me why I was making a fuss out of this and told me that he was not going to pay a cent towards our daughter's upkeep. He went on to say that our daughter needs to know how hard life can be and that she can't get everything handed to her on a silver plate, adding that she must know what suffering means.

This is coming from a man who lived for free in a company house, drove a company vehicle and still earned an additional 15000 to 30000 Rands a month, (that was 10 times more than what an average person earned). The reason for our divorce I will leave for another chapter!

Looking at my daughter's happy and sparkly eyes, I felt so sad that her dad did not even ask to talk to her. I hid my feelings and let my strength take over. I said out loud, "My daughter will continue to live the high standard of life she is accustomed to as long as she has me. She will live a good life without a struggle."

I wanted to look after my daughter on my own. My parents offered to take care of my daughter and me. However, I did not want to worry them about finances. They already had done so much for me when I was growing up, and I needed to become financially independent. My daughter was looking up to me and I wanted to be that strong and independent role model to her.

I had just moved to Canada and it was a new place for me, a big change of environment, but I knew I had my family behind me. I had determination, my reason being my daughter, and that force that was pushing me. Within a few months I got my first job, I enrolled my daughter into an early school program. It was the first time in my life that I learned how to handle money. I was a spoiled kid. My dad always bought me things even when I had a job and was married. Everything was always provided for me, from the latest cars to the latest fashions. But now, I had these beautiful brown eyes looking up at me and I was not going to let my daughter down. The love I had for her drew me to be responsible for the first time in my life!

**You Have All the Tools**

I never really experienced many challenges, but I believe it was because I remembered and followed the path of my influential ances-tors. During those first years in Canada, I learned to handle my finances from month to month. Yes, it was really hard as I had never understood the value of money. I did not borrow any money as my parents or granny never did. I would have moments when I thought I could not do this on my own, then suddenly my daughter would come running and giggling into the room, a whole burst of energy would come over me and my mindset would change immediately to 'YES, I can do it'. I had a reason to do this as I looked at her standing in front of me. Because of my daughter, I learned to put every example I was taught into practice. I would fill my sad days with prayer and my happy days with music and thanksgiving. Mum would repeatedly tell me to start saving money, she would say, "you just never know when you will need it." So, I started saving for my daughter's future. I would work three different jobs, often totaling 17 hours a day. I began to feel good about myself; I was becoming responsible by putting my daugh-ter's needs over mine, thriving at my jobs, and learning to save money. After several years, I was able to buy a house and fully furnish it. I paid for everything with cash and I was even able to put a big deposit on the mortgage and still had enough to add to the savings for my daughter.

**Blessed Beyond Measure**

God orchestrated my life so perfectly. God plans for every second of one's life to be fulfilled and happy. He brings unseen angels to guide us in life when we go off path. He connects us with the right people to teach us valuable things about life that cannot be bought with money. My family legacy taught me through the 5 people in my life as follows:

My dad taught me to be hard working, never to listen to negative voices and to walk in my calling in life in order to be victorious. He also taught me to be a businesswoman, stay focused on the vision and to put God first, (This stage kept me from all negativity in life and made me realise I have higher power. This gave me a powerful and peaceful mind). My mum showed me honesty and the importance of cleanliness and how to be a prayer warrior. She also taught me to be a career woman, to be happy and how to take care of the home (I learned to multitask and how to put things into order in everything I do. My grandma taught me to value, honor my parents and the importance of blessings from others. I learned compassion and to build relationships. My daughter taught me that unexpected things happen in life, but together we can hold each other's hands and rise together to be over-comers in everything. God gave me my daughter in order to make me financially responsible. My aunt taught me that even before I pray, God knows my needs and has already answered my prayer. All of these powerful people showed me the heart and thoughts of God, and how God never gives up on us!

Today I am an author, hold titles as a beauty queen, and have established my own community project called coffee of encouragement. I have created different groups for the following programmes: pregnancy care, human trafficking support, youth safety, bereavement/suicidal/addictions, body positivity, motivational & nutrition, women's purses care gift, care gift for prisoners, mental health and encouragement. I am also a businesswoman, an owner of a wedding empire and still have a full-time career.

Through the legacy passed down to me, I was able to create my own legacy. I discovered I am a visionary, a creator, a relationship builder, a humanitarian, a businesswoman, and a fearless woman. I am able to create projects, run them and still get to enjoy my life! Without a legacy you cannot live your calling. You need your legacy to strengthen you, find out who you are and what your purpose in life is. Your roots direct you in the way you should go.

My purpose to the story is that legacy is passed down and we add to it and continue it. My parents were involved in setting up and financing community projects. My grandpa created a community feeding program and I added to their dreams and made them bigger. I chose this path because it was destined for me. Everything in life pushed me to this destination of being a businesswoman and a career woman, a co-creator to what my legacy gave me and to add to it. I believe God chose us to be in the families we were born into in order to continue the legacy.

When you are on your right path and calling in life, you will always be blessed beyond measure, highly favored, filled with joy, and loved unconditionally. You can stand fearless always knowing that doors will open so you can reach and possess every dream you have inside.

I now know God is that powerful force that pushes me from inside. He is always with me.

Treasure the good and little things in your life, as this will eventually lead you to unimaginable huge blessings!

Yoleen Naidoo is a businesswoman, career woman, motivational speaker, philanthropist, author, body positivity/beauty and health coach, beauty queen, ambassador and a mum.

She has gained experience working as a business development associate, account manager and administrator with criminal, civil and maintenance courts. She recently completed training in Positive Psychiatry and Mental health, Social psychology, International Leadership and Organizational behavior.

She started her own community organization called coffee of encouragement inspired by her grandfather and parents who were actively involved in the community. It is through these experiences that has given her the skills to continually add value to her community. She was born in South Africa, now resides in Canada and enjoys building and supporting her community through channels, projects and campaigns she has developed. Her love for God and her family has inspired her to be an overcomer. Yoleen is passionate about raising awareness on human trafficking and empowering families.

Connect with Yoleen:

Email: yoleennaidoo@icloud.com

Instagram : https://www.instagram.com/yoleen.naidoo.9

Face Book community: https://www.facebook.com/coffeeofencouragement

Website: www.coffeeofencouragement.com

Manufactured by Amazon.ca
Bolton, ON

23330915R00081